Amrit

Mahinder

FOR KING AND ANOTHER COUNTRY
AN AMAZING LIFE STORY OF AN INDIAN WORLD WAR TWO RAF FIGHTER PILOT

'My story is a long one but it's not an ordinary story.'

Squadron Leader Mahinder Singh Pujji, DFC, PCS, BA, LLB, Honorary Freeman of the London Borough of Newham, Chairman of the Undivided Indian Ex-Services Association, UK, Vice President Nuclear Disarmament.

FOR KING AND ANOTHER COUNTRY:

AN AMAZING LIFE STORY OF AN INDIAN WORLD WAR TWO RAF FIGHTER PILOT

The recollections of
Squadron Leader Mahinder S. Pujji,
as recounted to Graham Russell

ARTHUR H. STOCKWELL LTD
Torrs Park   Ilfracombe   Devon
Established 1898
www.ahstockwell.co.uk

© *Mahinder Pujji, 2010*
First published in Great Britain, 2010
All rights reserved.
No part of this publication may be reproduced or transmitted in any form or by any means, electronic or mechanical, including photocopy, recording, or any information storage and retrieval system, without permission in writing from the copyright holder.

British Library Cataloguing-in-Publication Data.
A catalogue record for this book is available from the British Library.

Arthur H. Stockwell Ltd bears no responsibility for the accuracy of information recorded in this book.

This book is dedicated to Mahinder S. Pujji's late father, Sarder Sohan Singh, BA, LLB, superintendent, Department of Education, Health and Lands, Government of India.

ISBN 978-0-7223-4010-3
Printed in Great Britain by
Arthur H. Stockwell Ltd
Torrs Park   Ilfracombe
Devon

Words inscribed on a panel given as a present to Mahinder S. Pujji in September 2002, for his 84th birthday:

'You are a true pioneer in the family.
Your courage is unsurpassed.
Your generosity is experienced by all.
You have laughed and loved and created happiness amongst those around you.
You are a living legend and a source of inspiration to all.
We love you and are proud to have shared your life.'

CONTENTS

Foreword		9
Introduction		11
Chapter 1	A Soaring Ambition and a Desire for Adventure	15
Chapter 2	Fighting for the British	36
Chapter 3	A Hard Landing in North Africa	69
Chapter 4	Fighting to Protect the Empire	75
Chapter 5	Burma – the Biggest Test and the Finest Hour	79
Chapter 6	Amrit Is Waiting	102
Chapter 7	A New Fight for Survival	107
Chapter 8	Racing Against the Odds	111
Chapter 9	Forgetting the Past – Paying a Visit to Post-War Germany	139
Chapter 10	Heading for the West	170
Chapter 11	Epilogue	180
Chapter 12	Pujji's Family	182

FOREWORD

This is the story of the pivotal moments in the life – both personal and professional – of one of the most experienced war pilots alive today, as recalled by the man himself, Squadron Leader Mahinder Singh Pujji.

A detailed inventory of the Second World War operations he took part in will not be found in these pages – that kind of information belongs in logbooks. Instead, this work focuses on the recollections of Pujji himself. He reveals the experiences that, after distilling in his mind over the years, have risen to the top and taken on a special significance for him.

This book aims to give insights that no official record can rival, such as how it felt to prepare to leap from a plane in the pitch dark somewhere above the Channel, to crash-land in a desert, to dodge jungle treetops while searching for and strafing ground troops on a daily basis, to lose a close friend in battle, to miss the birth of your first child, to take tea with a young royal called Princess Elizabeth . . .

Interference from outside has been deliberately kept to a minimum. This is about how Pujji remembers his war and his life afterwards. Reams of information and opinion could be written on Pujji's difficult role in suppressing an uprising of the Hurs in his own country, the wider context of fighting in Burma and North Africa, meeting Nazi V1 test pilot Hanna Reitsch, even the rights and wrongs of wearing a turban in battle instead of a helmet – but this would dilute and distract from Pujji's words, which show his innermost thoughts, views and fears and suggest how a pilot who faced death almost every day for five years coped.

An abundance of quotations have been included from Pujji to bring the reader closer to the war veteran. They were gathered during a series of face-to-face interviews in a flat in Gravesend, Kent, accompanied by tremendous hospitality in the form of gallons of tea and orange juice and a small mountain of biscuits.

Including his own words adds striking insight and colour to past events, whether traumatic or amusing. Comments such as the following reveal much about the man: "Every flight, every operation was full of excitement and danger. Not a single comfortable flight – each time we were either shot at or had to run back home."

Note the word *excitement* occurred to him before the word *danger*.

In the copious pictures included in this book, Pujji often appears stern and unmoving, but his actions show the warmth of a man gifted with immense courage, purpose and willpower.

There are many Second World War heroes we should celebrate and honour. When thinking of Pujji, it is important to remember that he did not have to fight this war. Testing times can bring out the best in a man, but Pujji was prepared to sacrifice his life for the good of a country he had never visited and knew only as a colonial power. He responded to a call for help – and Britain and Britons are for ever indebted to him.

INTRODUCTION

Dense, tropical forest, suffocating humidity and continual rain – a new theatre of war presented a fresh challenge and a fresh enemy. A young RAF pilot named Mahinder Singh Pujji had read in the newspapers about the Japanese in Burma (now called Myanmar) while he was stationed in Miranshah, in what was then India. He wanted to go there, even though he knew it would be far more dangerous than his present job of flying Lieutenant General George Molesworth (the military secretary to the India Office) across the vast region. On 19 August 1943, with the General's permission, Pujji left the North-West Frontier Province behind and flew east across India towards Burma. From then until the end of 1944, Pujji would face death almost every day.

During the Burma campaign, he endured the most basic facilities. The airfields – Ratnap, Fenny and finally Cox's Bazar – had no control towers. Some didn't even have an established runway, with aircraft bouncing off giant steel plates laid on the soft ground instead. Far from enjoying the security of regimented barracks, the pilots had to make do with living and eating in straw huts, or bashas. There were makeshift arrangements for showers and toilets. It was almost as if the well-maintained aircraft upon which their lives depended were given more attention than the pilots.

"It was just good enough. We didn't expect anything better as we were fighting a war. Our attitude was not to look for luxury. I only wanted to fly," said Pujji.

The base was so deep in the jungle it could not be reached by road. An occasional brave driver would cut a path using a jeep, but otherwise the base relied entirely on airborne supplies. Once the day's fighting was over, there was no chance for weary pilots to catch a film at the cinema or enjoy a social drink at a bar to help them forget their worries and celebrate another day of life. In fact, the only outside contact came when a passing tribesman would appear and ask for food.

The conditions were the same in every base that Pujji was posted to during the Burma campaign. But it was in the constant rain of Burma, flying from Cox's Bazar just over today's Bangladeshi border, that Pujji's biggest test and finest moment came.

He was posted to No. 6 Squadron and then to No. 4 Squadron as flight commander. His mission, at first, was simple. Job one was to fly in a straight line over the tropical rainforest and take pictures of the ground using cameras mounted on the plane. Any images showing enemy movements would be passed to an army liaison officer as valuable intelligence to be used by troops on the ground, operating in the choking closeness of the jungle. Job two was to kill all Japanese soldiers in sight (they were usually spotted by telltale fires that would often provide their last meal).

"We killed them whenever we found them. I would look for smoke, then I climbed up and dived to attack them," said Pujji.

Burma proved to be one of the bloodiest conflicts Pujji experienced. The Japanese Air Force, known to him as 'Zeros', had superior aircraft and would regularly attack them as they flew on their reconnaissance missions. Every day, Pujji's thirty or so pilots woke up knowing they would spend several hours flying over the enemy in an airplane that was inferior to theirs. Air Marshal Sir Keith Park once told Pujji, "I appreciate you are fighting using aircraft which are second best." If you were shot down over the jungle, there was no chance of a safe landing.

"We were flying Hurricanes; their Zeros were like Messerschmitt 109Fs – far superior. If they saw us, we had no chance. We just had to use the aircraft we had," remembers Pujji.

Just two weeks after he arrived at the base, the second flight commander, an Anglo-Indian called Flight Lieutenant Reporter, was shot down and killed. In 1944 an estimated thirty-five pilots under Pujji's command were killed.

In a theatre of war that took such a toll, job promotions came rapidly. One day Pujji was flying alongside his commanding officer – a New Zealander named Sharp – and ten other aircraft. They were sweeping for Japanese forces. The task was made difficult and dangerous by the constantly low-lying Burmese rain clouds.

"We entered the clouds and when I came out on the other side I was the only person left. All my eleven colleagues were missing," said Pujji.

Left alone and vulnerable to attack, all Pujji could do was fly back to base. Once out of his cockpit, he scanned the heavy skies and waited. One by one the pilots came trickling in, but Sharp never appeared. They were sent out again to sweep the jungle for any signs of a crash site. Flying along the coast, Pujji found a wrecked plane on the beach. But by the time troops on the ground reached the spot the aircraft, and anyone injured inside it, had been washed away by the sea.

"That night no food was cooked at the camp and everybody was very upset," remembers Pujji.

The next day, Pujji became Squadron Commander.

Faced with the need to maintain morale in a battered squadron that was taking casualties daily, Pujji did what he did best – he flew. Every morning after breakfast the pilots would look at the orders for the day pinned to a makeshift noticeboard, listing who was to fly and when. And every morning the same name was first: Pujji.

Then came news that 300 troops under US command were lost in the jungle and running dangerously low on both ammunition and rations. With enemy forces approaching fast, the US commanders had sent out waves of search parties but to no avail. They came to Pujji – he was their last hope.

CHAPTER 1

A Soaring Ambition and a Desire for Adventure

Like most good pilots, Pujji grew up next to an airport. As such, his first great influence was thrust upon him. As a seven-year-old boy in Delhi, he would sit and stare as planes of all shapes and sizes took off and then he'd race over to see others land. It fascinated him for hours, as it would any young boy. It only became a true obsession when his older brother started learning how to fly.

Pujji was born on 14 August 1918 in Simla, a mountainous and beautiful area in Northern India. It served as the country's capital in summer, playing host to the entire Government of India as officials sought shelter from the sweltering heat of Delhi further south. Pujji's father, Sohan Singh Pujji, was a senior government officer in charge of education, health and land across the Commonwealth. He was the only Indian among a throng of British officers working in what was then a government of the empire.

Pujji's is not a rags-to-riches story. He remembers his childhood as a fortunate and comfortable one in which he enjoyed the many privileges of the upper middle class – a rarity for any non-British in India at the time. Because of the distinguished status of his father, his family could afford many luxuries, including one of the first cars in the neighbourhood.

"We would eat at dining tables and have proper times for lunch and have servants to serve us," said Pujji. The hardship would come later.

Perhaps the comforts he grew up with and became accustomed

to pushed him towards a life of adventure in tough conditions, carrying only the few personal possessions he could fit in his kitbag.

Their high societal status fostered a degree of separation between his family and the general population that Pujji only later became aware of. He grew up in a kind of enclave, living in areas exclusively populated by those working for the government. In those days the employer would provide everything, and a job was a job for life.

"We were very different from the Indians who lived in the towns and villages. Living in a metropolitan city was not like living in other places. It never bothered us because we didn't know any different," Pujji admitted. "We didn't feel Indian, we didn't feel English; we felt modern."

He was brought up surrounded by Anglo-Indians, meaning one of their parents was British. Although there was no social contact with wholly British families, their cultural influence pervaded his upbringing, sparking a fondness for the distant country and no doubt partly influencing his decision to dedicate his life to fighting for it in battle.

He was educated in the Kaithu area of Simla from the age of five, taking away from it a thorough knowledge of the times tables, which, he fondly remembers, would be sung out loud every day.

At the age of ten, he moved on to attend Sir Harcourt Butler High School. Created to serve the families of the civil service, the school moved every six months with the government from Simla to the recently established New Delhi. It was during this time in Pujji's life that a desire to be first, to prevail, and to excel at sport began to take shape. One of his first schoolboy memories is of becoming a class prefect. "You have to be the best to get that accolade," said Pujji.

There were plenty of sports at school and Pujji triumphed at every one of them. Be it the 100-, 220- or 400-yard dash, high jump, badminton or even pole vault, he would come first. He later won the district championships in badminton at the age of sixteen and represented his university in the pole vault.

Mahinder.

My father.

Pujji in a Flying Flea.

Pujji with colleagues from Himalayan Airways.

Pujji's family.

G. B. Singh (left) with Pujji.

Lachmi with her brother Dulu.

Manmohan Singh.

Pujji with his first car in London.

Pujji with a colleague.

Pujji awarded his RAF wings.

KING'S COMMISSION

The King's Commission appointing Pujji to the rank of pilot officer.

A letter from Valerie.

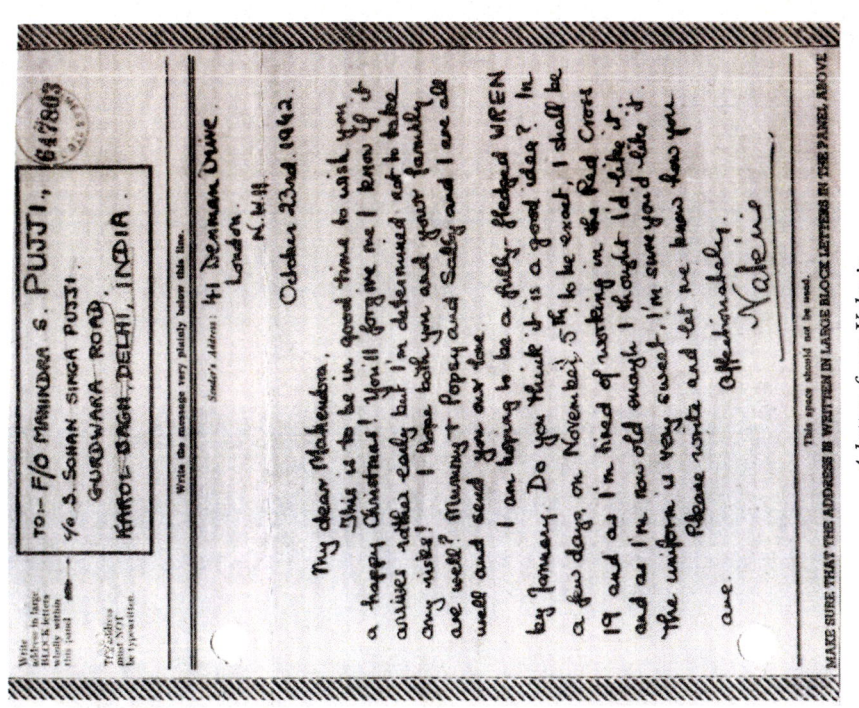

A postcard from Lachmi.

23

The Western Desert.

Cairo.

Skating in Cairo.

The Great Pryamid, one of the Seven Wonders of the World, Egypt.

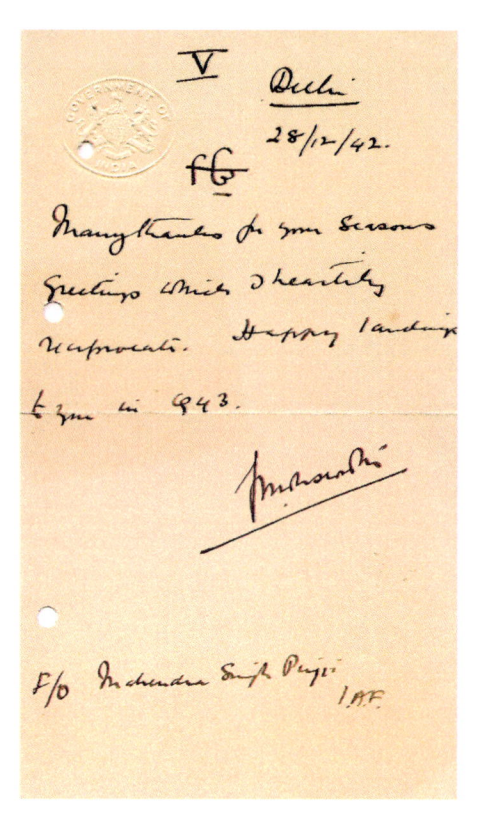

A letter to Pujji from his army commander.

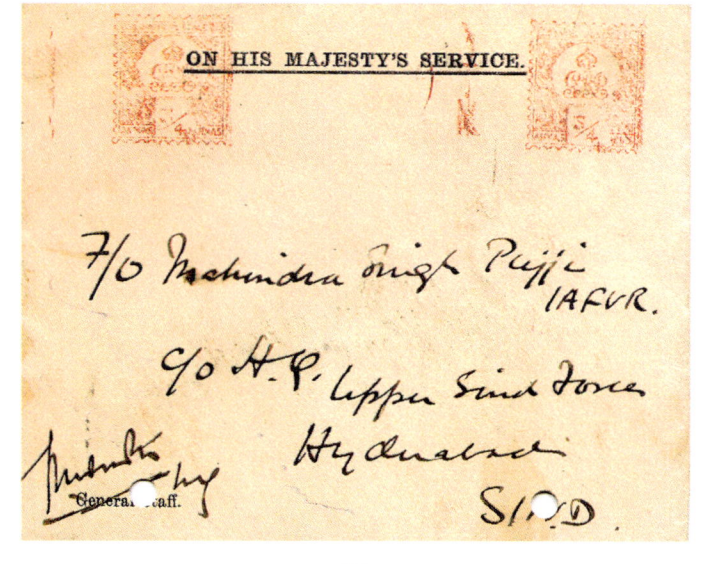

Palestine.

Amrit.

Burma.

The Pilots

"Scramble! Pilots dash for their aircraft on receiving the 'alert.'"

Flight Commander Pujji

Burma.

Flt. Lt. M S Pujji and Hurricane IIB.

Burma.

Burma.

Pujji's wedding.

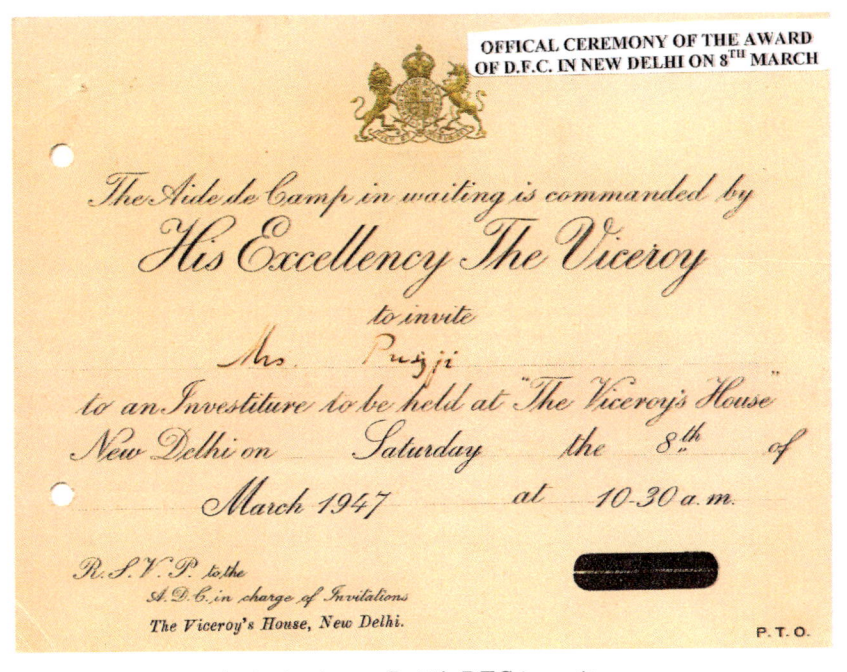

An invitation to Pujji's DFC investiture.

The letter of congratulations from Sir Keith Park.

In the military hospital at Kasauli.

PATIENTS & STAFF
of the
Lady Linlithgow Sanatorium
Kasauli.

Present

SIPAHI
(SOLDIER)
In Hindustani

Produced and Directed by
Flt. Lt. MAHINDRA SINGH PUJJI
D.F.C, R.I.A.F.

Story,   K. M. DURRANI, R.A.

Music,   Ch. PARTAP SINGH
         VERMA, R.A,

A play presented by patients at the hospital in Kasauli.

The only factor that affected which sport he played was the terrain. In the hilly pastures of Simla, it was not possible to play football and hockey.

Pujji's parents wanted him to do well in life, but they were not pleased with his athletic prowess. "Sports were not very popular with my parents or with anybody during that time," said Pujji. "We were always told we were playing and not studying. They wanted me to be academic. They only recognised academic achievements. They only felt happy about sport when I won the pole vault and it was covered in the newspaper. I just carried on anyway."

Still, English, geography and, particularly, modern history held a fascination for Pujji and were to prove essential in later life. No matter how hard he tried, any skill at art or drawing escaped him.

Pujji quickly made friends with like-minded people who enjoyed sport too, particularly badminton, and they would spend endless days playing. They were local boys and all the families knew one another. Firm friendships were formed with the likes of Kartar Singh, Sohan Dhiman, Rajinder Mathur and Mohinder Singh. All the boys went to the same school, so it was easy to stay in touch. Even now, Pujji remains in contact with them all and often wishes he had thought of taking pictures at the time.

Although he and his friends shared a common love of sport, studied at the same school and played in the same neighbourhood near the airport, Pujji found he was somehow different. He had different influences and desires working in him. Pujji recalls telling his friends for the first time that he was interested in flying. They were thrilled for him, but it did not go any further than that. Flying was an expensive dream and few could afford it.

As college beckoned, the group of friends saw less of one another. Many went on to reach important posts in adult life in India. Kartar Singh joined the army and later retired as a major general. Sohan Dhiman built a very successful factory in Jagadhri, north of New Delhi. Rajinder Mathur went into a career in the civil service and retired as a first secretary, or department head, in the Government of India. Mohinder Singh also retired as a first secretary (in the Foreign Office). Only Pujji ended up leaving the country, though he did not plan to at that time. Pujji said, "We never thought that we would go abroad. It never occurred to us."

In 1936, when he was eighteen years old, Pujji made the leap from dreaming about flying to doing it. But there was the problem of cost. By now Pujji's father, Sohan Singh, had retired and much of the wealth and privilege the family had previously enjoyed were gone. The family rented a modest house in the Boileauganj area of Simla, where daily life proved much more basic.

"Flying was very expensive. However high up my father had been, there were limits. I didn't want to burden him with more expenses," said Pujji. To make matters worse, one of Pujji's elder brothers, Iqbal, was already flying by this time and their father warned that he would not foot the bills for a second son to fly. It wasn't just aviation costs Iqbal ran up. "My father used to receive bills every month. There was always a problem with payment because of the drinks my brother took in the club. Every time he flew he took whisky too," remembers Pujji. His brother insisted that flying was too dangerous an activity to do without having a drink, but this irritated the younger Pujji.

"I told my father that he was paying more for drinks than for flying. I said, 'You let me fly and I will show you that I can fly without drinking,' and that's what happened," he said. It was the first of many upsets caused by Pujji's distaste for alcohol. He later irked many in the RAF by never touching a drop, preferring a glass of milk instead – hardly the drink of a brave fighter pilot, they thought.

So, to help with the costs, Pujji took a job with Himalayan Airways as a student pilot while studying at college.

There was, and still is, a roaring trade in ferrying Hindu pilgrims from Hardwar, the airline's base, to Gaucher Airfield in Badrinath, both of which are in the northern state of Uttarakhand. Badrinath has been a major pilgrimage site since the ninth century, and hundreds of thousands of pilgrims visit it every year. Hardwar – sometimes known as Haridwar, or 'Gateway to God' – is one of the seven holiest sites for Hindus. Pujji would fly three pilgrims at a time in a de Havilland Fox Moth airplane – a light aircraft for which he still harbours many fond memories.

With his flying hours stacking up for free as part of his work, Pujji qualified for his pilot's licence in April 1937, securing a full-time job the following year with the Shell Oil Company in Gwalior, overseeing the resupply of all airlines passing through India, including flying boats.

The job was a great opportunity, but it did not give him the chance to fly. As the months dragged on, frustration spurred a disgruntled, adventure-seeking Pujji to make a decision that would set the course for the rest of his life.

CHAPTER TWO

Fighting for the British

When the Second World War broke out, adverts calling for pilots to join the RAF appeared in newspapers in India. Despite the obvious dangers, Pujji saw only the opportunity to do what he had dreamed of – flying for a living. "It wasn't because I knew much about Hitler, but that I would be able to fly without having to pay for it," he admitted.

Pujji approached his British superiors at Shell, asking permission to volunteer. Keen to help the war effort, they said they would give him his job back, if he made it back. So he applied to the RAF and was immediately accepted, being awarded the King's commission on 1 August 1940.

But his excitement at his acceptance was tempered by the realisation he would need to tell his parents of the dangerous and faraway path he had chosen.

"My parents were devastated on hearing the news," Pujji recalls. "I still have a letter from my father saying, 'There doesn't seem any reason for you to do this. When you have a job being paid well, why should you risk your life?'" The response for Pujji was remarkably simple; he wanted adventure and he wanted to see the world. "I said, 'This is my future and this is what I want.' I was not scared but I thought then that I may not come back alive." His parents came to see him off at the railway station. "My mother was crying," remembers Pujji. "That's when I said, 'Why cry when I'm alive? You may have to cry when I'm dead.' I said to wait for that." It would be two years before he saw his parents again.

After securing his commission in August, Pujji's life changed very fast. In September he was put on a ship to England. After a long voyage – the pain of which was eased by his first-class cabin – Pujji and twenty-three others arrived in Liverpool in the dead of night. The Indian cohort was then placed on a train bound for London. Despite the late hour, they were welcomed by the Secretary of State for India, Leo Amery.

The arrival of this small group of foreigners – who had yet to receive any military training – was of hugely symbolic importance to the British people. Most national newspapers noted the event, using it to boost a public morale battered by the onset of the horrific continual bombardment of the Blitz.

"The reception overall was exceptionally good," recalls Pujji. "The next day, in almost every newspaper, there were photos of us, saying, 'The Indians have come.' On one photo, I remember, the heading was, 'They still wear turbans.'"

Such was the status of the newcomers that they were invited to take tea with the royal family at Windsor Castle (Buckingham Palace was off limits at the time, such was the threat of bombing). Pujji found himself sitting at an ornate table facing King George VI and Queen Consort Elizabeth Bowes-Lyon and nestled between the two young princesses, Elizabeth (14) and Margaret (10). "That was a real privilege. We talked a lot about India. Margaret was wonderful. She would ask, 'Where did you learn to fly? I thought in India they only had bullock carts?' And Elizabeth would tell her to stop being silly. Margaret also found my turban fascinating," remembers Pujji.

The group were billeted at RAF Uxbridge, famous for its pivotal role in the Battle of Britain and its links with a certain Thomas Edward Lawrence, better known as Lawrence of Arabia. Although it was an honour to stay in the West London station, its strategic importance meant it saw some of the heaviest bombing. But this rarely bothered Pujji, who lay awake full of anticipation.

"Our billets would shake every time a bomb was dropped. We couldn't sleep and I didn't want to sleep. I wanted to watch for the searchlights," he said.

Within two weeks of arriving in England, Pujji was lucky to survive a first-hand experience of the devastation the relentless German bombing campaign was wreaking. He was staying the night at the Overseas League Club in Piccadilly, Central London, when the building took a direct hit. "The building was on fire. We all evacuated and saw fire engines all over the place. That was my first experience," he said. The next day breakfast consisted of cold bread because the kitchens had been destroyed.

Travelling anywhere in the capital always provided stark reminders of the suffering the war was causing. "The Underground platforms would be full of people. They were sleeping there – people who had left their homes, or had no homes. It was very difficult to watch," said Pujji. He was struck by the fortitude and resolve of the British people. "Sometimes we would go to the movies. There would be an air raid every ten minutes and people were given the option of going to the shelters, but very few people would move. When I saw this, I thought, 'These people have very great courage,'" said Pujji.

Despite the horror of the Blitz, Pujji never once felt the urge to go home, although many would not have blamed him for doing so. As his father had pointed out, he had a well-paid job in India, where he could enjoy the delights of New Delhi and the rugged rural countryside of his birthplace in Simla, far away from the death and carnage in Britain. But, even if it did bother him, Pujji did not have time to reflect on the constant danger – the RAF had prepared a crash conversion course to teach him military flying. What was normally a two-year training course, covering everything from meteorology to armaments and navigation, was condensed into less than six months.

On 6 November 1940, Pujji and his fellow pilot hopefuls were whisked north to the Elementary Flying Training School in Prestwick, Scotland. The windswept base, with a two-mile stretch of grass for a runway, was their home for the next three weeks as they learned the military principles of flight. Every day, the previously civilian pilots would take to the skies in Tiger Moths –

a popular training aircraft with the RAF. Pujji also later flew American Harvards and the Miles Master – an advanced training aeroplane which proved to be a favourite out of the fifteen or so types of aircraft he used during his career.

December saw them sent to RAF Hullavington in Wiltshire, where Pujji encountered the machine he was to rely on for the next five years: the Hurricane. "That was something different," said Pujji. For the next four months, he honed his flying skills in the fighter, which was bigger and much more powerful than anything he had experienced before. But it presented a daunting challenge. The trainees had been used to aircraft such as Tiger Moths, which had room for an instructor in the cockpit. In a Hurricane they were alone. Every inch of space in a Hurricane was taken up by either the pilot or the fighting machinery.

"There wasn't a comparison between the two," said Pujji. "In a Tiger you get an instructor at the back. He won't let you crash. You can't do anything wrong. In a Hurricane there was no one to help you and about fifty to sixty instruments in front of you. I remember an instructor said, 'Can you take off?' I said yes, but in my heart I knew I was not sure."

Training aircraft and Hurricanes are different in one further small, but very important, respect, which Pujji discovered during his first flight. After take-off and ten to fifteen minutes of flight, Pujji began to relax, and he made preparations to land. As he started his descent, something on the ground caught his eye.

"I saw my instructors. They were all waving to me. I thought they were saying hello," Pujji said. "As I got closer to the ground they were frantically waving, so I went up again." To make matters worse, there was no radio contact with the ground. Pujji had no way of finding out what had scared them so much. As he circled around, Pujji flicked the switch to lift up his undercarriage. But the switch was already up. The heart-stopping realisation came to him that he had just tried to land without lowering his wheels. Tiger Moths have a fixed undercarriage so he had never needed to worry about it.

Coming around with wheels down, Pujji landed safely.

"Pujji, that was a narrow escape. We might have had to send you to India in a box," his instructor told him afterwards.

It was while training at Hullavington that Pujji lost his first friend to the war effort. "G. B. Singh was the first person I knew that died. He was my room-mate. One day, we were told he hadn't come back from a flight," remembers Pujji. It was at this point that Pujji displayed one of his more remarkable character traits, one that would keep him going through years of fighting with little or no rest – willpower. Once he had settled on how something should be done, he had a unique talent to see it through, regardless of the difficulty or danger.

"I would wake up at night and find the other bed empty. That gave me a feeling of sadness. That was the initial reaction I had. But I always understand why I am sad and then correct myself. It wasn't that I didn't have emotion. It was that I controlled it. I'm just like everybody else, but I used my willpower," he said.

This outlook also meant Pujji travelled through life, particularly in his early and arguably most vulnerable years of war, without looking to another celebrated pilot for inspiration. He supported himself entirely. "I have never had a role model in my life. I have never needed to look to anyone else for help," said Pujji. "It's a trait of my character. People often misunderstand and think I'm arrogant."

Having got to grips with the machine he would fly throughout the war, the next and final stage awaited. April 1941 saw him and his cohort taken to RAF Sutton Bridge in Lincolnshire, where they would cover entirely new ground. The training would bring them closer to the reality of war – how to engage and destroy enemy planes and troops.

Taking to the air at the Operational Training Unit, they began by firing at simulated targets on the ground before progressing to air-to-air training, firing real rounds during exercises with fellow trainees. "You had a camera fitted in every aircraft so you can see it all on-screen later. In the classroom we were told where we had gone wrong," said Pujji.

But all too soon the training was over and the exams were passed. In April 1941, Pujji, along with seventeen colleagues, was awarded his RAF wings. Within a year, twelve of them were killed as they fought in the skies above Britain.

By now Pujji had visited, and flown over, many parts of Britain. Was he horrified by our customs, our ways? Far from it. And was he still prepared to die for us? His answer was a resounding yes. "In general everything in this country I like. The way I was treated was wonderful. I couldn't believe there was no discrimination," he remembers. He soon found out why.

"Firstly, the RAF uniform was a big thing," he said. "People were always keen to please me because of the uniform, and especially because of my turban. I was different from others. That was probably another attraction – something which surprised me."

One time, the film *Gone with the Wind* – a recent release back then – was showing at the local cinema. It was proving very popular and, when Pujji had an evening away from training, he left the family home where he was billeted and went to see it. But its success proved a problem, because the queue out of the cinema stretched for hundreds of metres and it was starting to rain. Pulling up his military overcoat – he had no umbrella – Pujji joined the back of the queue. All of a sudden, the man in front of him turned round and said, "Sir, you don't have to stand in a queue – you're fighting for us." Pujji was quickly ushered to the front of the snaking line, with not a single grumble or complaint from those he passed.

He now faced the girl in the booking office and, still bewildered by his treatment, asked how much it was for a ticket. The girl looked even more surprised than Pujji. She studied him for a few seconds, to check if he was joking, before saying, "You don't have to pay – you are fighting for us."

Remembering these moments, Pujji said, "These things, they captivated me in a way. The people were so loving, so friendly." He remembers thinking that when he retired he would love to

41

come and settle here. At the time, he didn't realise how prophetic that thought would prove.

Pujji found the English abundantly honest too. One afternoon he made a telephone call in a public booth but accidentally left his wallet there. He did not realise he had lost it until that night. The next day he began retracing his steps and eventually ended up at the booth, knowing that it could not have lain there for more than a day without someone making it their own. He looked inside the booth and, sure enough, it was nowhere to be seen. Crestfallen, he noticed a nearby shopkeeper looking at him. The man called out, asking if he was looking for somebody. Pujji explained that he had lost his wallet. The man disappeared into his shop for a minute and then returned with the missing wallet. "I thanked him, but the man said, 'Don't thank me. There was a guy who found it after using the phone and left it with me,'" recalls Pujji. "So there wasn't just one honest person, there were two."

He remembers being surprised at the lack of discrimination. It did exist, but not in the way he expected. He bought an Austin car during his training days in 1940 and would spend much of his free time driving around the countryside, but one day a lack of planning and the restrictions of petrol rationing – four gallons a month – meant his car stopped dead in the middle of nowhere. Abandoning the vehicle, he wandered up a country lane and knocked on the first door he came to.

The voice of a woman drifted through the door, asking who was there. Pujji remembers saying, "I'm sorry, I have run out of petrol. Can you help?" In a swift reply the woman said no and told him to please go away. Desperate, for he had no way of getting home that night, he knocked again and shouted, "Sorry, I'm not from round here. Please tell me where I can get help!" She opened the door and, as soon as she saw the turban and the uniform, her tone changed dramatically. She said, "You speak very good English. I thought you were an Englishman so I told you to go away." If Pujji had been born and bred on these shores, he would have had a very chilly night in his Austin.

As it turned out, he was given the standard English welcome of a cup of tea, and the woman's poor husband was sent out to get petrol from the nearest station. "Why wouldn't I fall in love with a country like that?" said Pujji after recounting the experience. Even the weather didn't bother him. He was quite happy with an overcoat to protect him from the biting cold of his first British winter, even when he spent time in Drem, in Scotland. Pujji puts it down to a youth spent at 8,000 feet in the mountains of Simla, where it was cold at night and snow fell every winter.

The only sticking point was the food. He just could not stomach it. Little did he realise at the time that this would prove to be a recurring problem and it would nearly cost him his life. The only meal he could bear was the English breakfast – or at least a part of it. Every morning he would order a hearty feast of sausages and his favourite drink, milk. But he would refuse both lunch and dinner. This did not go down well in the households he was billeted with during training. As an officer, he was placed with families of some standing, and the expectation was that he would dine, and behave, as one of them. It was with some reluctance that the cook was asked to make him breakfast for all three meals. He was also chastised for opting for milk at every opportunity instead of something a little stronger. He was told, "Only children take milk in this household," but he eventually got his way.

However, the line was drawn at his attire for breakfast. One morning he came down the stairs in a dressing gown and was politely informed that he had to turn up properly dressed if he was to have anything to eat.

Expectations of his behaviour also stretched beyond the confines of the household. The lady of the house would vet his choice of evenings out and which dances he should go to. "She said, 'No, don't go there – officers don't go there. I will tell you another place.' So that class thing was there, and, being a commissioned officer, I was considered one of them," remembers Pujji.

Throughout his experiences of making new friends in the new

society he was part of, Pujji never forgot why he had come to England, and now that he had his wings he was eager to make his mark. His flying skills had impressed during his training assessments and he was chosen to become a fighter, rather than bomber, pilot. From then on he would proudly keep the top button of his tunic undone, to silently broadcast his new status. "We wanted the public to know we were fighter pilots. That made the difference," he said.

In June 1941, he got his wish and was assigned to No. 43 Squadron. His moment had come, but his hopes of getting into the thick of it were dashed. They had just finished a stint as Britain's line of defence and were resting. Pujji was so disappointed that he applied for a transfer; he was sent to No. 258 Squadron the following month.

He spent six months with them, based at a spartan airfield in the village of Kenley, near Croydon, Surrey. Indeed, it was such an unassuming place and so well camouflaged that Pujji found it difficult to find it and land after his first sortie. But, almost a year after leaving India, Pujji was now in the hot seat and ready to contribute to the war effort.

The tour consisted of four principal missions: convoy patrol, escorting bombers, interception and occasional sweeps of enemy territory. When the alarm sounded, he and his fellow airmen would rush to confront whatever threat came from across the Channel. "We had to run for the aircraft, take off in less than one minute and meet the enemy in the air," said Pujji.

Wheeling over the South Coast, his first dogfight was a vicious but triumphant affair. Amid the noise of the engine, the mad rushing of the wind and the cacophony caused by the machine guns, he thought he had shot down two Messerschmitt 109s.

Pujji landed in Kenley, glad to be alive and jubilant at his victories, but he was to be disappointed. He explained: "Every aircraft is fitted with cameras, and when you fire, the camera works. When they developed the film they said, 'You didn't kill those people; you only fired at the aircraft,' so they didn't give me the credit for the kills." Nonetheless, he was off the mark in what would prove a long and grim war.

From the outset, wit, skill and luck saw Pujji through. On two occasions in the first six months a charmed Pujji escaped an untimely end.

Flying at 20,000 feet over enemy-held territory in France one day, a hail of bullets suddenly smashed his dashboard to smithereens and sent engine oil arcing across the cockpit, completely obscuring his vision. He didn't realise it at the time, but a round had also punched through his heavy leather jacket, missing his body by an inch. Controlling the stricken plane as best he could, he banked and made for home, unsure if he had seconds or minutes before his plane became an uncontrollable lump of metal a very long way from the ground.

Many of his instruments were broken, and the engine began to grind and stutter owing to the lack of oil. The situation was so serious that Pujji broke radio silence to let the control room know he might have to bail out over France. He was advised to try to make it to the Channel, where a rescue effort could be more easily launched.

Soon his Hurricane became little more than a very heavy glider. It began its inexorable descent. Time was running out. Pujji was down to an estimated 8,000 feet now, but he could make out the shimmer of water below. He was making progress, and every mile he could squeeze out of the plane before ditching was a mile closer to home. Then a horrific realisation hit Pujji.

"I was about to jump out when I looked at the sea below. I didn't want to bail out. It was cold and, more importantly, I didn't know how to swim," he said. He relayed his fears to the control room, and a very understanding young woman at the other end reassured him they would pick him up as soon as possible. But a frantic Pujji now felt he had a new reason to use every bit of his flying skill to try to make it to land.

A source of great hope and inspiration to many, the White Cliffs of Dover, loomed into view, and an encouraged Pujji radioed for details of the nearest airfield where he might perform a crash-landing. Things were looking up. Gliding powerless a few hundred feet above the ground, Pujji spotted the airfield and made preparations to land. Congratulating himself for remembering, Pujji flicked the switch to swing the undercarriage down. He was promptly engulfed by flames. "I couldn't see anything. I only knew I was 200 feet up. But by God's work I crash-landed at the airfield," he said.

Everyone on the ground had been put on standby to rescue him from his damaged aircraft, and what they saw as he approached resembled a vision from Hell. The Hurricane-turned-fireball landed and came to a crunching rest upside down and burning fiercely. "Then I heard lots of people," Pujji recalls. "I had my eyes closed because of the fire, but I heard many people saying, 'He is still alive,' and they dragged me out. When I put my hands on my turban it was full of blood."

After his miraculous escape, Pujji spent several weeks in hospital being treated for serious head injuries. His turban had saved his life, but it hadn't been easy persuading the authorities to allow him to wear the traditional headdress of his homeland.

Pujji's attitude to his turban was always one of practicality and tradition rather than religion. He wore one simply because that was how his parents, whom he greatly respected, had raised him. "I was brought up as a Sikh and my father was a practising Sikh. He would go to the gurdwara in the morning, and I would often accompany him. We were together in prayers, but there wasn't anything inside me that said I should pray," he said.

Despite the incredible dangers of his new profession, religion simply did not appeal to Pujji – although he had nothing against those who held a belief. His view was that it was something to be practised privately. Throughout his life he made Hindu, Muslim and Christian friends, but the subject of faith was never discussed.

As a pilot, Pujji was spending hours every day in his combat uniform, and he was dismayed at the prospect of spending time putting his turban back on every time he removed his helmet. "It irritated me that I would have to tie it back up. There's six yards of it," he said. "So, when I flew, I insisted on not taking off my turban." Pujji pleaded with his officers, saying it was against his religion and explaining that the tightly wrapped cloth was as good as a helmet anyway.

To his surprise and delight the authorities relented. Even the problem of earphones – which are designed to fit around a helmet, not a turban – was overcome. A special strap to fit around the turban was developed, tested and given formal approval. He flew with other Sikh pilots, but Pujji claims to be the only pilot to fly in the air force without removing his turban.

It acted as a protective helmet and saved his life on that occasion in Dover, but there were many other times when he thought he would not live, with or without the headdress.

Pujji was on a routine patrol when his squadron was suddenly confronted by enemy planes along the south coast. The British Hurricanes scattered in every direction to get a better angle on the German Messerschmitts. The attackers were seen off but the danger remained. After the confusion of a dogfight was over, a pilot would radio in to the control room to be guided back using the innovation that was radar technology. But, after hours of circling in the darkness, using up valuable fuel, Pujji could raise no one on his headset. "I had to get home, but suddenly I found there was water below me. I was very low over the water, but my height was about 18,000 feet. Then I realised I was over some kind of mountain range," he said.

Confused, Pujji tried to reach the control room again for a fix on where he was. There was no answer. It slowly dawned on him that he must be a long way from home and out of range. With strict blackout regulations in force, there was no way he could spot a nearby airport, field or other suitable landing spot.

More searching proved fruitless. He simply could not work out where he was, and he could find nowhere suitable to ditch. As the fuel gauge dropped, Pujji began to make preparations to bail out. "I gave control my details, which you don't normally do, and gave my life story. I thought that was my end. I wanted them to tell my parents in India that I had a wonderful life here and died for a good cause," he remembers.

He also left instructions for his body, if it was ever found, to be cremated in England rather than sent home. There was still no response from control. Pujji climbed high to give himself the best possible chance of opening his parachute, although what he would land on was anybody's guess.

With his fuel tanks practically empty, time had run out. He released the cockpit canopy and braced himself against the rush of freezing wind that threatened to tear him out of the plane like a rag doll. He put one foot up on to his seat, but his second foot caught in the radio cord which was still attached to his earphones.

He scrambled down to unplug himself but thought it best to radio his latest position to secure the best chance of being found by rescuers. Suddenly a voice came through loud and clear, shouting, "Don't jump! Don't jump! You are not very far from the airfield."

Pujji described the response from nowhere as 'a very pleasant shock', but there were still problems to overcome. "I said to them, 'Thank you very much, but I have no petrol and won't be able to fly any more. I can only glide," Pujji recalls. He still had no idea how far away or in which direction the airfield was.

The control room then took the bold decision to switch on their searchlights, which formed the shape of a cone, and they told a struggling Pujji to simply head for the lights. It was a move that immediately made them a very prominent target for any enemy planes in the area. To Pujji's relief, his route to safety blinked into view. He landed safely and the runway lights were extinguished.

Climbing out of his cockpit, he was greeted by the commanding officer. A quick check of his fuel tanks revealed they were bone dry. "The officer told me I was the luckiest person he knew," remembers Pujji. Then he asked the officer which airport he had landed at. He was told RAF Drem, but he did not immediately recognise the name. It was in East Lothian, twenty miles east of Edinburgh, Scotland, and more than 400 miles from his home airfield.

Veena.

Pujji as an aerodrome officer.

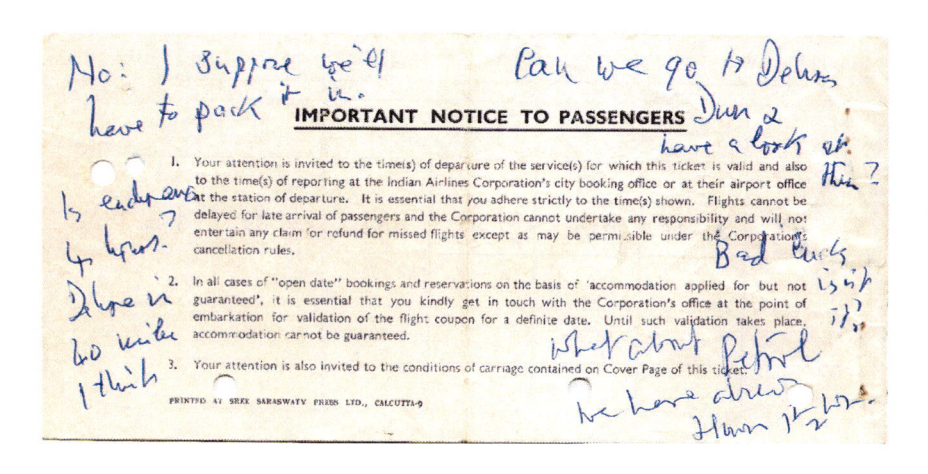

A flight ticket written on by Group Captain Leonard Cheshire.

THE RYDER CHESHIRE FOUNDATION
for the Relief of Suffering

Founders :
GROUP CAPTAIN LEONARD CHESHIRE, V.C., D.S.O., D.F.C.
SUE RYDER, O.B.E.

In association with :
The Cheshire Foundation Homes for the Sick

Cables : CHESHOME Dehra Dun

Raphael,
16, Pritam Road,
Dehra Dun, U.P.
Tel : 217.

16th Jan

My dear Piji,

Herewith my cheque for Rs 47:11, together with my most grateful thanks.

We are planning our own landing strip on the river side; it shouldn't be too difficult. That will be the day, won't it?

With all best wishes,
I am v. sincerely
Leonard Cheshire

A letter from Group Captain Leonard Cheshire.

Pujji with USSR President Brezhnev.

A letter of congratulations from General Cariappa.

Pujji and his family, pictured after his success at the 2nd National Air Race.

Pujji with Amrit, the naval chief and Brigadier Vikram Singh.

Pujji and Amrit with his trophy, 2nd National Air Race.

Pujji and his brother in Assam with the naval chief.

Pujji received by the Governor of Assam.

Pujji with the Governor of Assam.

Delhi Gliding Club.

Pujji with Amrit.

Pujji with Edwina Mountbatten.

Squadron Leader Pujji takes Lady Edwina Mountbatten of Burma up in a glider

Pujji with Lady Pamela Mountbatten.

58

Pujji's lady students.

Prime Minister Nehru and Surinder Gill.

Pujji with Prime Minister Nehru.

THE INDIAN EXPRESS

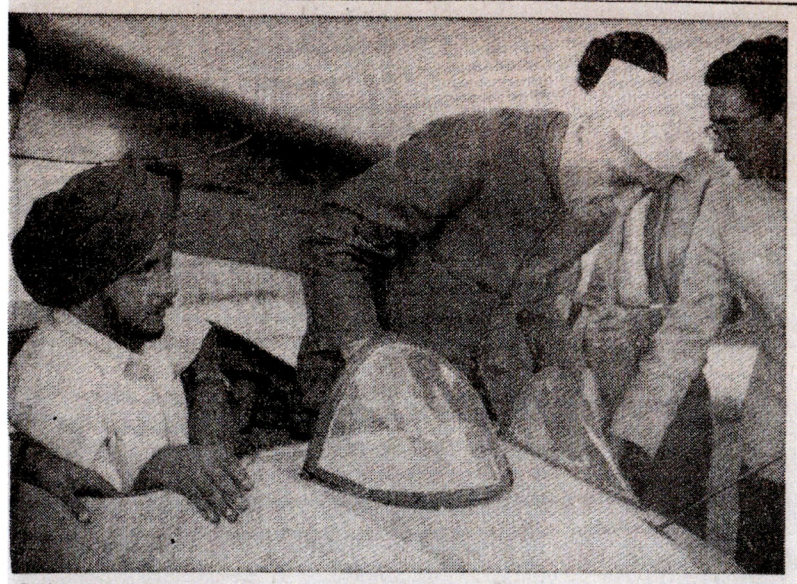

During his routine Sunday afternoon off, Prime Minister Nehru gave a surprise visit to the Delhi Flying Club where, after inspecting a French plane, he dodged the security police and got into a glider for a short joy ride. Picture shows the Prime Minister getting into the glider.

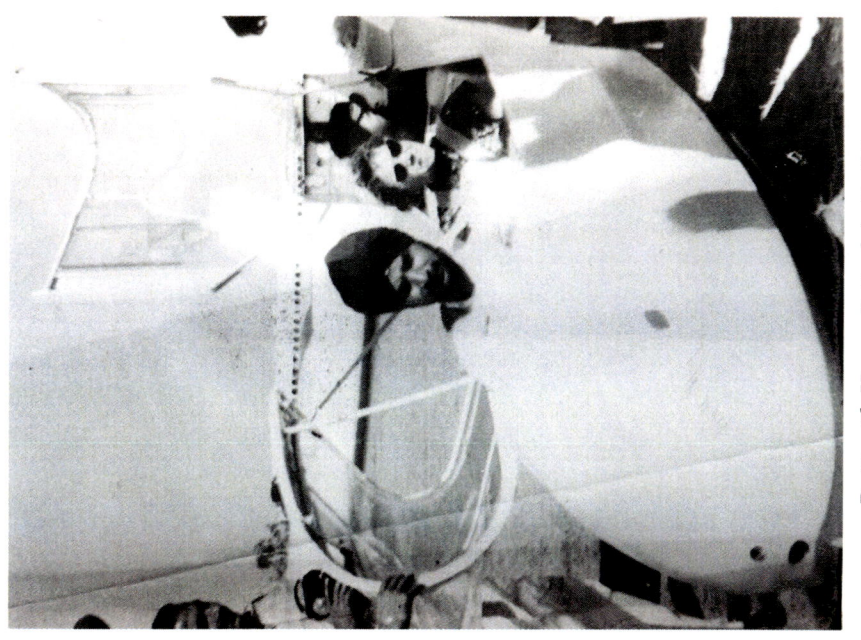

Pujji surprised by Prime Minister Nehru.

Pujji with Hanna Reitsch in Delhi.

Pujji chatting with the Queen about his visit to Windsor Castle in 1940.

Pujji with Prince Philip in Jaipur.

Meet the Queen and Duke of Ed...

Pujji with the Queen and Prince Philip.

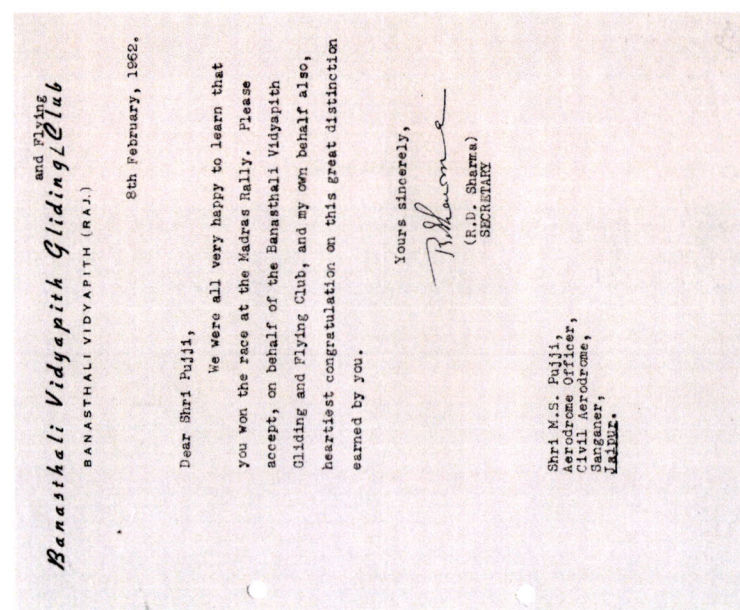

Congratulatory letter from the Gliding and Flying Club, following Pujji's success in the 3rd National Air Race.

The Govenor's wife presenting Pujji with the trophy for the 3rd National Air Race.

In the course of one night, Pujji had wandered almost the entire length of Britain.

Meanwhile, back home in India, all Pujji's parents could do was watch. As a member of the first batch of Indian pilots to volunteer and fly for the RAF, Pujji attracted a lot of attention from the media. He found the spotlight was focused on him because, out of the group of twenty-four pilots that underwent training, Pujji was one of only six chosen to become fighter pilots. Indeed, when he returned to visit his family in 1942 he was asked to talk at a series of public engagements, including a presentation entitled *A Pilot Officer's Diary* on All India Radio.

"My parents would see me in the news in the cinema. My photo was shown many times, which my family saw," remembers Pujji. But the newsreels were far from comfortable viewing for his mother and father. Eighteen Indian pilots from the first cohort qualified to fight in the RAF, but twelve of them were killed within a year. Pujji was one of only two pilots in that select group to survive the war.

Pujji did not realise at the time just how dedicated his family were to keeping in touch with him. They had not left him to his fate thousands of miles away. They had not tried to forget him, dismissing him as the wayward son who gave up a stable life in India to search for foolish adventure. His mother, Sant Kaur Pujji, was most affected. Every day she would go to the cinema and pay to see a film she would never watch. She went only for the news bulletin shown at the beginning of the film, praying she would not see the coverage she feared most.

She must have wondered what she had done to have sons that caused her so much worry. After Pujji joined the RAF, his four brothers joined the armed forces in India. Teja Singh became an accountant with the Indian Air Force – which later became the Royal Indian Air Force – while Iqbal joined up as an aerodrome officer, in charge of Karachi Airport. Amrik Singh joined the navy and would reach the rank of adjutant general – the only Indian officer among a sea of British faces at the time. The youngest brother, Kulwant, completed the set by joining the army engineers as an officer. All the brothers were proud of what Pujji had achieved.

Pujji would often write to his family, and soon a stream of letters was passing twice a month back and forth across the globe between New Delhi and Kenley. Reading the notes from his parents must have seemed like an exquisite form of torture – in every letter there was the pleasure of hearing from them but also the ever present paragraph in which they would say they were praying and hoping he would come back soon. Pujji had to be firm. 'I may not be coming back, because civilians and pilots are being killed here,' he wrote.

Perhaps to show this grim reality to his faraway parents, Pujji took out a subscription for them with the *Daily Mirror* – which was then a hefty tome of a newspaper filled with accounts of each campaign – so they could keep up to date on every development in the war. The attitude of many people in India, and of the Indian Government, was that it was not their war. It was not something they should be involved in. Only in November 2007 did the Indian Government officially recognise Pujji's efforts in the conflict, more than sixty-seven years after he left to fight for Britain.

But what his family could not read in the newspaper was that Pujji was beginning to develop more of a sense of purpose as a pilot. He realised he was there not just to fly around in powerful planes for free, but to win a war. He grew to despise Hitler more and more. This was no longer just a game.

This new-found determination and change in mindset was inspired not only by seeing the daily devastation of war around him, but also by the British reaction to it. He never failed to be impressed by how the man or woman in the street simply accepted the fact that they might wake up to hear their street, their friends, being torn apart by bombs, or that they might never wake up at all. "The public was wonderful in the sense that they accepted the onslaught of German bombers and they just carried on," said Pujji. "I had a real sense of duty and I admired the courage of the English people."

Even more inspiring was the reaction of those on the front line – his fellow pilots. Pujji has always felt a strong sense of duty, and the pilots he flew with every day shared that resolve – a trait he respected. "The pilots would go two or three times every day to fight with the Germans and never did they all come back. They were so brave and dedicated for their country," he said.

However great his dedication to Britain, Pujji could not fight on an empty stomach and he relished every opportunity to sample a taste of home at Indian restaurants. It was during one of these evenings, at a restaurant called Shafi in Piccadilly, that he was reminded how much of a curiosity he still was to Britons.

He was eating his dinner when a man asked if he could join him. He said yes, and soon the man was practically interviewing him, asking Pujji's opinion on the country he had decided to fight for. "I said the only thing I didn't like is when it's dark at night and I walk home, girls on the street say, 'Hello, hello, come with me.' I said this was very bad, but he laughed," said Pujji. The man that had been so curious turned out to be Dr Vivian Meik, an author and diplomatic correspondent to newspapers *The People* and the *Sunday Post*.

After the meal, Dr Meik asked him where he was staying. Pujji said Uxbridge and the journalist offered to give him a lift there and take him to meet his family – his wife and young daughter – along the way. Pujji was struck by the modesty of the daughter, Valerie (17). Her nature reminded him of girls in India. Pujji struck up a close friendship with both Valerie and Dr Meik that would last throughout the war. In a letter to Pujji, dated 14 July 1941, Dr Meik wrote, 'Do keep in touch so that I shall know at all times where you are.'

Having nearly completed his first six-month tour, Pujji had explored and gradually come to understand Britain. He had fought for its society and been proud to do so because of the people – pilots and civilians alike – he had met. He had developed an immense respect for the way of life here, even if the cuisine was not generally to his liking. Pujji had settled in. But when his training and first tour came to an end, everything changed. He was offered some well-earned leave, but he decided not to take it. Pujji was then sent to the Middle East at the end of September 1941. Within a week he had exchanged the mild climate of England's south coast for the searing heat and choking sand of the Western Desert to join the fight against Rommel.

CHAPTER THREE

A Hard Landing in North Africa

The contrast could not have been more stark for Pujji. If he thought the conditions were tough in Britain, what he faced in North Africa plunged off the scale. Every aspect of life was a struggle in the inhospitable terrain. Comfortable billets in Uxbridge were exchanged for primitive and draughty tents; the temperate West European climate turned into the sticky daytime heat and night-time chill of the barren desert. Instead of fending off German attacks at night, they came by day. Suddenly, Pujji had to shield, rather than strain, his eyes to spot his quarry. And the enemy, who were winning the war at the time, had a plane that was on a par with Pujji's. In short, his world had been turned upside down.

Following its development before the war in 1934, the famously rugged Messerschmitt warplane morphed into ever more powerful models, with increasingly impressive weaponry mounted at each step. By now, Pujji was facing wave after fearsome wave of the Messerschmitt 109F. "We knew they were superior to us in some areas," remembers Pujji. "Hurricanes were much slower than them. They produced aircraft easily as good as ours."

But a devastating event thousands of miles away changed the war entirely, giving the Allies a new momentum in their brutal campaign in North Africa and elsewhere – Pearl Harbor. On 7 December 1941, several hundred Japanese planes launched a pre-emptive strike against the US Pacific Fleet sheltering in Hawaii. More than 2,400 Americans were killed, six battleships were sunk and 164 aircraft were destroyed. Declaring it 'a day that will live in infamy', US President Franklin D. Roosevelt entered the war.

In the same week, the ships that had escorted Pujji and his boys to North Africa – the 'invincible battleships', *Repulse* and *Prince of Wales* – were sunk in the Mediterranean in another Japanese onslaught. "That shook us. We had come to know the crews so well," said Pujji.

At a time when a lot of British blood was seeping into the sand, the news that the world's most powerful country had become an ally provided a much needed boost. "That made a difference to us. The US pilots joined us in the desert in large numbers. It was very good for morale," said Pujji. It was also a valuable opportunity for Pujji to indulge his love of new challenges and mastering new planes. The US forces brought their aircraft – B51s, B52s, Tomahawks and Kittyhawks – all of which piqued his curiosity. As part of a cultural exchange, the friendly forces gave each other the chance to fly the war machines of their nation – although not on operations.

Despite the entry of US firepower into the war, the daily struggle for Pujji and his fellow pilots remained as hard as ever. There was the wait, wondering what that day of relentless heat and blowing sand would bring. They would spend hours trying to ignore the simple fact that, on average, one or two of them would not come back each day. Then all hell would break loose as the control room scrambled them, usually two or three times a day, to fend off an enemy attack. Dogfights were the norm, planes wheeling and fighting over huge expanses of nothing.

Armed to the teeth with multiple machine guns, waves of one or two dozen Messerschmitts would regularly break over the Allied forces. At times, there were so many littering the sky that Pujji could not count them.

During Pujji's tour in London, he had the distractions and attractions of the capital to keep his mind far from the day's trauma, but out here there was nothing except a distant horizon that would only reveal another attack. The food that Pujji had enjoyed back in London – his three square English breakfasts a day – was nowhere to be seen here. "The only thing available was bully beef and 'dog biscuits'," said Pujji. "Beef I don't take and that left me with biscuits, and they were so tough you needed a hammer to break them." For three months, the Indian pilot fighting in a British plane against the Germans in North Africa lived on a diet of biscuits soaked in tea to make them edible.

It was while severely weakened from a poor diet and the stress of fighting daily for his life that Pujji faced his toughest desert challenge. During the course of yet another dogfight, Pujji's engine was hit. After coughs and splutters, the exhaust pipes quickly fell silent. The sound of other dogfights faded into the background as the sound of the whistling, buffeting wind grew. "The engine had conked out and I knew immediately that I wasn't going to be able to come home," Pujji said. With no idea where he was – navigation, after all, came after you won the latest skirmish – Pujji had to swiftly prepare for a crash-landing. With characteristic good humour, Pujji saw it as an easy manoeuvre. After all, there were no hills, only relatively soft dunes. "I came down comfortably, in the sense I had no fear compared to the other one in England," he remembers.

He guided the plane safely to a crunching halt on the ground and paused to get his breath back. He had escaped without injury. After briefly celebrating the fact that he hadn't created a fireball and hadn't needed to bail out, the reality of his situation dawned on him. He was stuck in the desert in a desolate expanse that gave him no clue as to which way was home. After the hectic noise of battle faded, a surreal quietness descended, giving Pujji ample time to contemplate what on earth he was going to do.

It was broad daylight when he was brought down, and the heat was unrelenting. Pujji had little to protect him from the elements, particularly the chill of the night if he was not picked up soon. He was confident his unit would soon realise he was missing, but would they be able to get to him? Would they have his last position and would they have the resources to come and look for him? All these questions, and many others, swirled around Pujji's mind as he sat beside his craft.

"In the end, because I couldn't see anything for miles around, I thought, "Do I have the capacity to walk one to two hundred miles?" I knew I was going to die, so I didn't worry about it," said Pujji.

By this point in Pujji's war, he had seen so much death that the prospect of his own almost seemed like just one of those things that could not be helped. After all, it was something that was happening to an awful lot of servicemen every day, so why should he be spared? "I had walked in the desert with bodies all around. Rommel was attacking us, and there were so many casualties. We got used to it so much a friend asked if I wanted the watch on a dead body," remembers Pujji, who rejected the offer.

Pujji may not have realised it at the time, but his preparedness for death may have proved a saving grace. It meant he rarely acted in fear. He never shied away from the thought of his own end during the war – he had made peace with it. He knew what he was doing. He had made a decision to find adventure in life, and here it was in all its bloody, dangerous glory. He had no regrets.

Squinting against the sunshine, the young pilot debated what to do. "All I knew was that if I headed north, I would hit the Mediterranean Sea eventually. In the end I just sat on top of my plane and took off my shirt because it was slightly blue so I could wave to attract attention if need be," Pujji recalls.

After several hours surrounded by little except his own increasingly despairing thoughts, Pujji saw a dust cloud rising high into the air. It was the answer to his prayers, he thought. He knew the cloud must be caused by troops, and, by that point, Pujji didn't care if it was friend or foe; he would at least get out of the desert and stand some chance of survival. Having made the decision, he stood on top of his wreck of a craft and swung his shirt above his head.

He was greeted by a reassuringly British uniform and accent

as the army column pulled up beside him. He hopped into a spare seat on a truck, leaving his stricken aircraft behind. He later found out that the troops were pulling back from the front line in the face of an enemy offensive. As Pujji bounced back along the desert path towards civilisation, he realised he had never been so happy to see his own forces in retreat.

When his new-found Army friends saw Pujji's condition and were told about his biscuit-and-tea diet, they sent him straight to hospital. It was a bitter blow for Pujji, who was quite content to, figuratively, fly himself into the ground, but there was no other option. He was transferred to the nearest medical centre, in Cairo, the capital of Egypt.

The hospital trip could well have saved Pujji's life. He was so exhausted and physically and nutritionally deficient that he was kept in for several weeks. A vital factor in his recovery was the food on offer. The meals available were not so different from the Indian cuisine he loved so much, so he was at last able to eat properly. To his relief, the hospital appeared to be a bully-beef-free zone.

Pujji enjoyed his stay immensely. He was back in a city alive with activity and bustle, a far cry from the desert wastelands he had called home for the past three months. He was able to refresh himself with new sights and sounds after the daily monotony of scouring mile after mile of empty sand. He was able to let go slightly, because he knew he would not have to scramble to meet an enemy patrol at a minute's notice. As willing as he was to meet that life-or-death challenge, back-to-back tours with little proper food had taken their toll on Pujji.

News must have soon spread of Pujji's stay in Cairo because the increasingly iconic British Indian pilot attracted his second royal reception. Once he had recovered, a relative of ruling monarch King Farouk I came to see him and took it upon himself to help rehabilitate and entertain his celebrity casualty. Pujji still treasures a photograph of himself sitting on a camel with the Great Pyramid in the background – one of many snaps taken during one of their numerous tours.

"That was a great time. The King entertained us. It was because we were fighting for the British. At the time I think Egypt was helping them," remembers Pujji.

Although there were none of the dances that he enjoyed so much in Britain, Pujji was soon able to enjoy other pursuits, such as the slightly less dignified pastime of roller skating.

The recovering pilot was also treated to visits from old friends from the Western Desert's front line. Because he was staying at an army hospital, it was easy for his colleagues to find him. They would often come in while enjoying a cherished few days' leave in Cairo on a weekend. It gave him a valuable boost, a tangible link to the reality of what he was doing in this part of the world. It also gave him something to aim for when he was well enough.

But Pujji was never sent back to the desert. He was instead promoted to flight commander, and, without even being asked, he was posted to the Afghanistan border – a place that was proving a terrible graveyard for pilots.

CHAPTER FOUR

Fighting to Protect the Empire

For generations, tribal fighters in the mountainous border region between Afghanistan and what was India but is now Pakistan had a fearsome reputation. Nothing had happened to change that when Pujji arrived at his station in India, five minutes from the border.

For some pilots, this tour might have seemed a difficult one from an ethical point of view. The tribesmen had not sided with Hitler to attack a British colony, and they were practically Pujji's countrymen, but, to his mind, they were simply taking advantage of the war to rise up against the ruling power. They were therefore fighting against what Pujji had pledged himself to protect. There was little room for moral dilemmas in a flight commander's mind.

"The important thing was that they were a hindrance to the war effort," said Pujji. "They were attacking British officers. Although they were not directly connected with the world war, they were harassing and killing officers – that is a serious threat. The war was an opportunity for them."

His job was brutally simple. As Pujji explained, "Wherever we saw any tribesmen we were supposed to kill them." The enemy was a fairly primitive force with no warplanes. They had only rifles to take potshots at Pujji and his pilots from easy-to-spot vantage points on hilltops. They should have been as lambs to the slaughter. But, as Pujji prepared himself for his third tour and the new role of flight commander, he received a sharp reminder of the kind of fierce fighter he faced out there. "One of our pilots was shot down by a tribesman. He was captured and killed and cut into pieces. They put it all in a sack and sent it to Pujji personally with a note saying, 'This will happen to you if you try to confront us.'

"It was done to frighten us – and it did," said Pujji. He realised it was only a chance bullet that had brought the hapless pilot down, but the consequences of one piece of bad luck or a minor error had now been explained very clearly for every pilot to see.

Pujji arrived at the posting in the border town of Miranshah, North Waziristan, in March 1942. Again, the facilities were basic. There were no buildings, other than temporary accommodation at the airport itself. Again, Pujji and his boys permanently wore their flight gear, ready to scramble into their planes at a minute's notice to support ground troops in the area.

Three times a day, Pujji flew to their British-built-and-controlled advance base in Razmak, South Waziristan, to refuel. Each time the trip to the makeshift strip, hollowed out of the surrounding forest, was fraught with danger. This was the place where the pilot had been shot down and his body defiled. His plane had been vulnerable as it dropped altitude to land. The area was swarming with tribesmen, and the surrounding hills gave them the perfect opportunity to chance their luck.

Despite many scrapes, Pujji made it through the first half of his tour without a crash-landing, but the killing was remorseless. Every day – in a mission brief that might seem brutal and out-of-place nowadays – Pujji would look for tribesmen, find them and destroy them.

Pujji had just finished his third month in this war of attrition when a call came through. He was to be transferred to take over from a flight commander that had been killed in Hyderabad Sindh in what is now Pakistan. In July 1942, Pujji packed his bags to fight in theatre of war number four.

His new mission farther south in Hyderabad Sindh was cruelly similar to the mission of the previous three months: find the enemy and kill them. This time he was ordered against the Hurs, a Sufi Muslim population that had risen up against British rule and was attacking forces under the command of Lieutenant General George Molesworth.

"We had many enemies. The Hurs would kill any white men they could find, wherever they found them. And because I was wearing the uniform, they would not spare me either. We would fly a couple of times during the daytime looking for them in the desert; and if we found them, we tried to kill them," said Pujji.

Lysanders were the aircraft of choice here. Bigger planes, they had room for a gunner in the back seat to strafe forces on the ground. They also enabled a pilot to take VIPs wherever they needed to go. There were no commercial flight services at the time, and Pujji often found himself trusted with a very important cargo: Lieutenant General Molesworth himself. It was from Pujji's Lysander that the General would gain an accurate picture of the enemy's positions as he flew between army bases. The tour must have made an impression on the leader because he wrote a personal letter of thanks to Pujji.

In Hyderabad Sindh, Pujji was reminded that, even in his own country, he was an outsider whenever he wore a British military uniform.

On a rare night out, he chose to go to the local cinema. He parked his military car and went inside. Once he had enjoyed the film, he came out to find his car burning in the street. He immediately ran over and began to beat at the flames. No one helped him.

"I managed to extinguish the flames. Someone had put a swab with kerosene in the car. Fortunately, the car still worked," said Pujji.

He jumped in and sped back to base before any more reprisals came his way – or indeed a visit from the military police. "We were not supposed to go to the cinemas," explained Pujji. "In every town in India the forces were not allowed to mix with civilians. I knew I would be in trouble with the authorities if they found out and asked why I went there."

Pujji had the damage repaired, and he survived without anybody raising an eyebrow. But the feelings of many local residents had been made clear: Pujji was a stranger and was therefore despised. The incident typified hostile feelings in India towards the world war as a whole, Pujji remembers.

"Some in India were opposed to the war. Others were just passive. But we were in the forces – we were with the British authorities so we were the enemy," he added.

Indeed, Pujji himself wanted independence from the colonial power. Iconic leader Mahatma Gandhi was as much a source of wisdom and pride for Pujji as for any of his fellow countrymen. But it was the Mahatma's peaceful request for Britain to leave India rather than a violent call to arms that Pujji sided with. After all, he felt there was much the colonial power had done for the country and he rejected the notion that Britain had been an oppressive power.

Through his father's job and the education he received, Pujji had come into contact with the British more than most. The straightforward approach of the colonial rulers appealed to him. They were no-nonsense, practical and entered into little debate on any issue, much like Pujji himself.

"We had a high regard for the British in every respect. Whatever was done was done by the British; and we appreciated that, whether it was law and order, transport, or anything that required a system," said Pujji.

He remembers that in his hometown of Simla the mountain roads were so narrow only one vehicle could pass at a time, often leading to bottlenecks and delays. "The British introduced a wonderful system of making the road one-way for two hours at a time. The system was good," said Pujji.

But Pujji did not have long to ponder his status as an outsider. He was required to fight, and, before long, he was sent east to face a new enemy.

CHAPTER FIVE

Burma – the Biggest Test and the Finest Hour

Pujji faced a fresh challenge in Burma and a fresh enemy – the Japanese. Working from a basic airstrip and living in a straw hut deep in the jungle, accessible only by air, Pujji was truly immersed in the conflict. The only contact with anyone outside the squadron would come if a passing tribesman appeared and asked for food.

It was here that Pujji's biggest test and finest moment came. He had been promoted to squadron commander after his commanding officer, a New Zealander named Squadron Leader Sharp failed to return from a sortie. The squadron had been battered by the Zeros and Pujji did his best to raise morale – posting his name first on the flight rota every day he was on duty.

"I always put my name right on the top because I wanted to be the first to face the Japanese fighters. I was not just going to send the boys to be killed," said Pujji. When his turn came, he would regularly fly the maximum number of flights possible – usually six flights in a day. This meant he would fly more than sixty separate sorties a month, which was a record, racking up more than 250 hours of flight time.

Two months passed since Sharp's disappearance and life under Pujji's command at the camp returned to its routine of daily sweeps and interceptions. Then, one day, a man appeared from among the trees on the edge of the forest and walked into the camp. It was Sharp.

After the pilots had recovered from seeing a 'dead' man walking, Sharp told Pujji an incredible story. He had got into trouble after being separated in the heavy cloud and had to bail out of his plane. He pulled the cord but his parachute did not open. He said his prayers and waited for death. But fortune smiled on him that day and he landed on trees that broke his fall. Alerted by the commotion, tribesmen came to investigate and found the stricken pilot. Given the reputation of some tribesmen, Sharp could have been forgiven for thinking he had jumped out of the frying pan into the fire. But they rescued him, treated his wounds and nursed him back to health in their village.

Weeks passed and a stronger Sharp realised he had no idea where he was. And the time soon came for him to pay his dues – in holy matrimony. He spent nearly two months married to a tribal girl before he ran away and eventually stumbled upon a British patrol that brought him back to base. Pujji marvelled at the story but lost contact with him after he went to hospital and then back to New Zealand. The newly promoted Pujji continued in his position.

As leader of No. 6 Squadron Pujji saw his past life in India and his new life as a fighter pilot overlap. One day a pilot named Inderjit Bhatacharji turned up for duty. He was an old college friend of Pujji's. The two were overjoyed to see each other again, though they were, of course, surprised at the unlikely reunion in the middle of a Burmese jungle. Inderjit flew under Pujji's command for some months before he was shot down.

"Naturally I was very sad, knowing his family very well. In schooldays we knew each other well and each other's families were close," said Pujji.

Inderjit was seriously injured, and he was flown back to India to be near his family. He was to spend six months in hospital. It was frustrating for Pujji to have lost an old family friend and a link to his home. He couldn't even see what medical progress Inderjit was making because of the huge distances involved. As quickly as his friend had appeared, he was gone.

The constant sorties and growing expertise in the difficult terrain were to set Pujji in good stead for what he sees as his greatest

A family picnic at Amritsar.

The winners of the 3rd National Air Race.

Pujji's family in Amritsar.

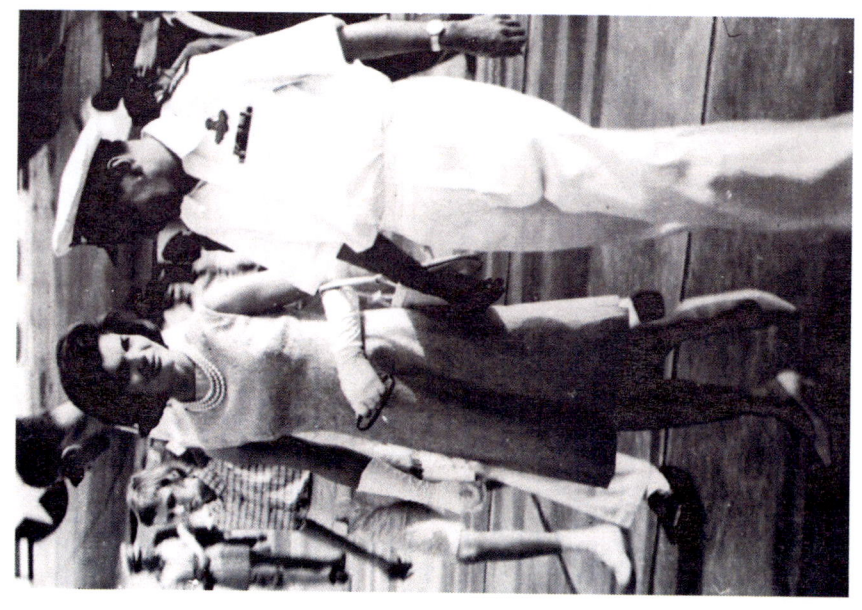

Pujji with Jackie Kennedy.

Pujji with the Maharajah and Maharani of Jaipur.

Pujji with Prime Minister Nehru.

Pujji with Prime Minister Nehru.

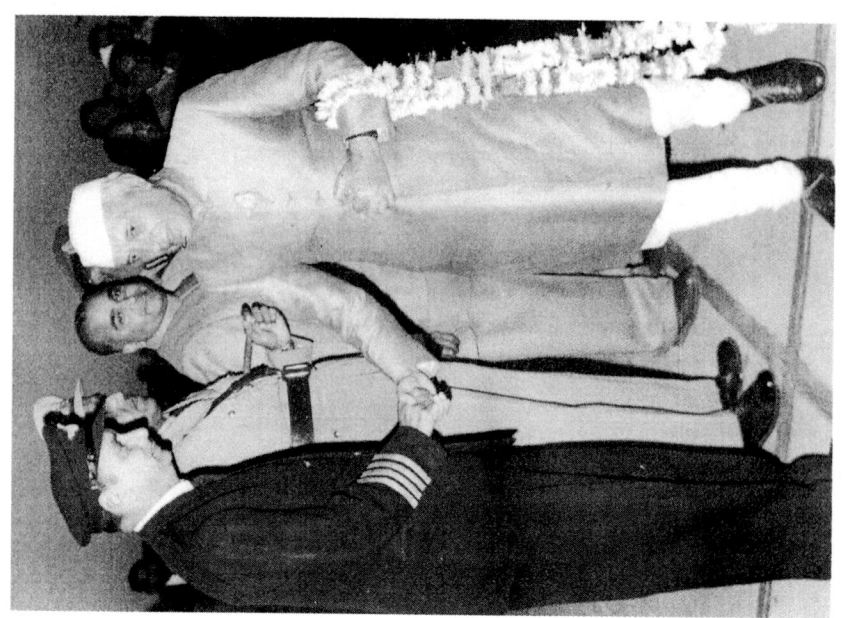

Pujji with Prince Philip and the Maharajah of Jaipur.

Pujji with Prince Philip and Maharajah of Jaipur.

Pujji in his glider, about to attempt the Diamond C.

Pujji in his glider about to attempt the Diamond C.

Pujji with the Aga Khan.

Pujji with the chief minister's wife and Prime Minister Indira Gandhi.

Pujji with Prime Minister Indira Gandhi.

From:- Air Vice Marshal H.Moolgavkar, MVC
VI.S.1112/16/AirOps HEADQUARTERS WESTERN INDIA
I. A. F. GHORUPDI
POONA-1
24th October, 1967

Dear Mohinder,

I am writing to thank you for all your help and the co-operation given by your officers and staff during Exercise GARJANA-I. The success achieved, to some considerable extent, can be directly attributed to this. It was quite clear that the unstinting manner in which all the help and consideration was given made our stay and operations at Santa Cruz during the Exercise indeed pleasant.

Thanking you, again,

Yours sincerely,

Shri Mohindar Singh Pujji
Aerodrome Officer
Santa Cruz Airport
Bombay-54

A letter of thanks from the Indian Air Force.

PUJJI WINS AIR RACE

TRIVANDRUM, March 8 (PTI).

MR M. S. PUJJI won the Nehru Trophy in the National Air Race which ended here today when the seven competitors landed their aircrafts at the Trivandurm airport one by one between 12 noon and 12.15 p.m. today.

The weather in Trivandrum was not bright as the six Pushpaks and one Piper reached here after a ...short halt at Peelamedu airport near Coimbatore.

A large crowd which had collected at the airport cheered the pilots as they came out of their planes.

Mr Pujji won the race for the second time in succession having been victorious when it was last held in 1962 in Madras.

Mr Pujji, who is 49, is senior aerodrome officer in charge of the Santa Cruz airport at Bombay.

He told newsmen at Trivandrum airport that his plane did not "behave properly" on the last leg, but he "just managed it".

In a close race, Capt. Bijoy Kumar Bahadur, flying instructor of the Bihar Flying Club (Patna) was second, 10.5 minutes behind, while only 3.5 minutes separated him from third-placed Mr R. S. Mann of Northern India Flying Club, Jullundur.

The other four pilots were ranked in the following order: Mr G. S. Bolina (Northern India Flying Club, Jullundur), Capt. P. P. Tikka (Hind Flying Club, Lucknow), Mr M. S. Ramachandran and Mr P. K. Ravindran both of the Kerala Flying Club.

The air race began on 3 March when the seven took off from their respective aerodromes. They converged at Nagpur on 5 March covering a distance of about 1,005 miles on prescribed routes in the first leg.

In the second and concluding leg of 941 miles, the pilots took off from Nagpur on 6 March and arrived in Trivandrum today after two night halts at Hyderabad and Bangalore.

'Pujji Wins Air Race'.

> Rashtrapati Bhavan,
> New Delhi-4
>
> I deeply appreciate and greatly value your kind congratulations and send you my heartfelt thanks.
>
> Zakir Husain

A letter from President Husain of India.

Pujji with the President of India, Zakir Husain.

Pujji after winning the 4th (and last) National Air Race.

Farewell party.

Farewell party.

Satinder leaving for the USA to study.

Convent of the Poor Sisters of Our Lady

TEL. 212009

"STEPHEN HALL"
23. WODEHOUSE ROAD
BOMBAY 1, INDIA

February 24, 1968

Dear Mr... Mrs. Pujji,

    In addition to the enclosed Invitation Card I am sending you this personal letter to say how happy and grateful I will be if you honour us with your presence at the Inauguration of our Divine Child School at Andheri.

    Awaiting a favourable reply, and with kindest regards,

Yours gratefully,

M. Patricia, P.S.O.S

(Mother Patricia Frank, P.S.O.L.)
Superior General

Letter to Pujji from the convent of the Poor Sisters of Our Lady.

Pujji visiting the Divine Child School at Andheri as guest of honour.

258 Squadron R.A.F. Reunion
will be held on Saturday, 27th. November, 1976
at
The Victory Services Club
63/79, Seymour Street,
London. WC2 2HF

Tel: 01 - 723 4474

Nearest Tube Station: Marble Arch (Central Line)
Bus routes: 6, 7, 8, 15, 16, 36

6. 45 p.m. for 7. 30 p.m.
Tickets (including Buffet, Wine, Service & V.A.T.) £4. 25

Limited overnight accommodation is available at £3. 50 per person in shared double room. Write direct to The Victory Services Club to obtain a booking.

KEEP THIS SECTION

258 Squadron RAF reunion.

258 Squadron RAF reunion.

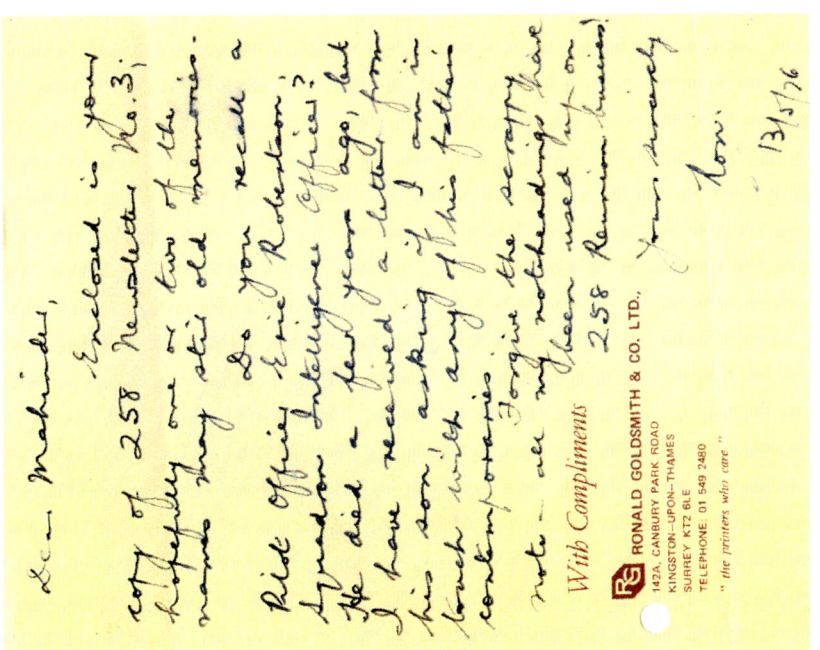

Amrit's brother Kaka and his wife Chani.

Hang-gliding.

Hang-gliding.

Pujji parachuting.

Pujji's first TV interview.

Pujji with Group Captain Leonard Chesire, VC, DSO, DFC.

achievement. In September 1944 he heard that some 300 troops under US command were in trouble, lost in the jungle. Three days had passed and nothing had been heard from them. Their supplies would be running low. The US Air Force and the RAF had launched several missions to try to spot them on the ground, but all attempts had so far failed.

It was then that Pujji was paid a visit by British Field Marshal William Joseph Slim, who was in charge of the 3rd Tactical Air Force Eastern Command, in support of the 14th Army in Burma. Slim was to revolutionise jungle fighting tactics by resupplying troops using airborne drops. He passed on a desperate US request that Pujji and his 'boys' seek out their lost troops. They were their last chance, Pujji was told.

Pleased that the request had finally been made to him, Pujji immediately sent out waves of patrols to scour the jungle, searching for evidence of any large troop movement. The brief was difficult and dangerous for the pilots. The flights had to be conducted during good visibility, making the pilots vulnerable to attack. In a Hurricane aircraft there was no room for an observer. The pilot had to simultaneously manoeuvre the aircraft at high speed and peer into the jungle with his own eyes. Altitude was crucial too. If they flew too high, the dreaded Zeros were scrambled and Pujji's pilots faced being shot out of the sky. But if they flew too low, either the treetops or a Japanese rifle might put an end to their mission and their life.

Despite three waves of paired patrols and a twelve-hour search, the pilots came back with nothing. Pujji decided to see for himself, alone. "They were all unsuccessful, so I decided to go. But I didn't go with a second person because I knew I was going to take risks and didn't want another pilot to be with me and be shot down," said Pujji.

Taking off in his Hurricane, he decided on a new tactic. He embarked on a wide detour over the Indian Ocean, avoiding the jungle where the troops were most likely to be. Having skirted the theatre of war, he banked and flew back very low towards the jungle – from the Japanese side. Pujji's reasoning was that he would have to fly incredibly low to spot anything, and so he would be sure to come under attack from Japanese ground forces. But he hoped the fact that he was flying from the Japanese side would make them hesitate long enough for him to be out of sight before they could bring their rifles to bear.

Flying just feet above the treetops, Pujji soon spotted columns of Japanese soldiers – some patrolling and some cooking. Having caught them by surprise, he was tempted to open fire, but he reminded himself of his mission. Eventually Pujji noticed a clearing in the jungle – usually a sign of some kind of activity. He circled but saw nothing. His hopes of ever finding the men began to fade, but still he circled.

"I must have done about ten or fifteen circuits. I was curious because I thought there must be somebody there – Japanese or friendly," said Pujji. Cautiously, one, two and then a dozen troops entered the clearing, squinting up at his plane, and began to wave.

Pujji's perseverance and conviction had resulted in troops from the missing 300 coming out into the clearing, he later learned. After the first few circuits the Americans were still not sure if he was friend or foe, but as he kept circling they eventually spotted the RAF markings on his plane and came out.

They had been found, but the next task was even more difficult. As he skimmed the jungle, he wrote a note, put it into a message bag, took careful aim and flung it towards the clearing. If he had missed, his bag might have stuck in trees, frustratingly out of the reach of the troops.

"That required all my flying skill. If I made a slight mistake, I hit the treetops," said Pujji. His message asked them to signal to him what they needed most. Using special strips of material, which they arranged on the ground to form huge letters – such as 'R' to indicate rations – they told Pujji they had run out of ammunition and food but that their most immediate need was a radio to communicate with their base.

Having received the information, Pujji then took another gamble.

He had spotted a Japanese column less than half a mile away from the troops' position. Without any ammunition they would be helpless, and for them to be captured, or worse, after he had found them would be terrible news to bring back to camp. 'So near and yet so far!' he thought, remembering the moment he found Sharp's wrecked plane. He scribbled a second note and dropped it into the clearing, warning them of the danger nearby.

A jubilant Pujji raced back to Cox's Bazar and proudly rang Field Marshal Slim to tell him he had found the missing soldiers and to give him their location. The next day, the joy turned sour. He got a message saying the US Dakotas that went out to resupply the beleaguered soldiers had looked in the location he had given them but had found nothing. Pujji was told that either he had given the wrong co-ordinates or they were not there any more.

"It gave the impression that they didn't believe me. That was a challenge," said Pujji. The only thing he could do was to lead the US planes out there personally. His aircraft was much slower than the Lightning two-seater aircraft they planned to use this time, so he arranged to leave four to five minutes before them. For the second time, Pujji flew out and found the troops. He circled at treetop level – that was the signal to the supply aircraft behind him.

Here Pujji remembers with pride that one of his pilots was H. Moolgavkar, who later became the Air Chief Marshal of the Indian Air Force.

Following his success, Pujji was nominated to attend the Military Staff College course in Quetta. This was an honour. He was the first Indian Air Force pilot to be nominated. If he passed, he would become a member of the Services Selection Board, which recruited commissioned officers for all the three services.

Having fought in the skies over four years and completed five tours of duty with barely a pause for breath, he walked away from his Hurricane expecting to return soon. But Pujji never flew a plane in combat again.

Counter to Pujji's expectations as a young pilot in search of adventure, he had not died in a fireball falling from the sky while desperately trying to defend his newly adopted country. After years of not knowing whether to bother making any plans for the future, Pujji was suddenly confronted by many decisions. It felt like the war had institutionalised him. Living, and celebrating, day by day was no longer necessary. And he was young – having only just turned twenty-six. Many might struggle to come to terms with a sea change in their life and prospects, but not Pujji. He was clear about what he wanted to do.

Like many doting mothers, Pujji's had often asked him when he was going to get married – even before he left for England, when he was barely an adult. Over the years, Pujji had become adept at fending off the enquiries, but they started to carry an ever more desperate tone.

In his hometown, Pujji had grown up with a tight group of both male and female friends. There was no one-to-one dating in those days, he remembers. Everyone went out in a group. And Pujji had always enjoyed that, until one day in 1943 when he came home on two weeks' leave from operations in Afghanistan.

He was greeted warmly by his mother, but the inevitable questions about when he was going to choose a wife soon surfaced. Pujji trotted out the same response as he had done for years: "When I find a girl I like, I will get married." But this time his mother was prepared – she had a photo of a prospective bride ready for him to look at.

"My mother took out a photo and said, 'How about her?' When I saw the photo I threw it back and said she looked like my auntie," remembers Pujji. "Then she started crying. She said, 'He will not get married because he can just hang around with girls instead.'"

Her emotion and the barbed comment hurt the battle-hardened but still-young Pujji. For the first time, his mother had questioned his character, and, for a man like Pujji, that was particularly painful. He did not want to see her so upset, yet he was not prepared to be forced into a marriage simply to please others. As a kind of gesture of goodwill, Pujji repeated his promise that he would say yes to marriage as soon as he saw a girl he really liked.

What he did not tell her was that he later arranged to meet the family of the girl in that photograph, even though he had not liked the picture. He staggered his journey back to the front line and went to meet her. He was allowed a little leeway – by this time, he was a senior officer.

It was the best decision Pujji ever made. She really was prettier than a picture, beautiful and charming.

"Her name was Amrit. She was a student in a government college in Ludhiana in Punjab. And when I saw her, well, I knew that she was the right girl. I was very fond of her. She was a lovely girl," said Pujji. "I told my future father- and mother-in-law there and then, 'I like this girl. You better ask if she likes me.'"

The two potential lovebirds were brought together in her family home for the chance to talk to each other alone. There was a spark between them, and, in the space of a three-day break there, Pujji got engaged.

But it was 1943 and he had yet to survive months of further fighting, against the tribesmen in Hyderabad Sindh and the Japanese in Burma. It marked a change, however slight, in Pujji's mindset. He remained as committed as ever to his cause – indeed, his finest moment was yet to come in the steaming jungles of Burma – but he now had a woman waiting for him to come home safe. Amrit wanted to marry straight away, but Pujji had resolved to see his war out first. "I didn't want to marry her and then make her a young widow," he reasoned.

His fellow pilots might well not have noticed any change in Pujji after his secret detour had it not been for one very public gesture to his wife-to-be.

Until now, his 'beloved' had been his cherished aircraft, catchily named ZTB B3518. Pujji managed to combine his two great loves by asking permission to write the name of his fiancée on his fighter plane. It was a visual reminder of why he must strive to survive the conflict.

CHAPTER SIX

Amrit Is Waiting

Once it was confirmed that Pujji's war was over, he sent a telegram to his father to give him the news. In reply, he received a letter from his brother, Amrik, an adjutant general in the navy:

My dear Mahinder,
   The most unexpected thing has happened for us! We are all thankful to the Almighty that he has heard our humble prayers and has given us hope of seeing your dear face again. Ever since the receipt of your telegram bring us the happiest news of the year, every one of us here is always talking and thinking about how to receive you and in what way to best express his or her feelings of joy, which know no bounds. We hope to all be present at the time of your arrival and will give you the best possible reception within our means. You should write to us first thing on landing, so that we may give vent to our feelings, which are at present a bit restrained because you are not yet out of danger. Mother is so bewildered with happiness but she doesn't easily express her feelings lest something may still happen to you. She will not be relieved from this suspense until your safe landing.
   I don't know whether this letter will reach you in time before your departure for Delhi. I may be too late but I thought I should put in a word or two of my feelings, which I could no longer restrain. Here we are so impatient (expecting your arrival every moment) that most of us would have come to Bombay had we known the exact date of your landing.
   I have just inquired from my wife whether she would like to put in a word or two but she says that she feels too shy to express her

feelings of joy and may I convey her sat sri akal to you, so here is sat sri akal to you from her.

More when we meet.

Yours affectionately,

Amrik

Travelling back from his Burma tour, Pujji arrived in Colombo, Sri Lanka, a free man determined not to keep Amrit waiting any longer. It had already been two years, and a thousand battles, since he first fell in love. He immediately sent a telegram to his father in New Delhi advising him of his imminent arrival and asking him to arrange a simple wedding ceremony.

Upon receiving news of the double celebration of his son's return and marriage, Pujji's jubilant father either forgot about the word *simple* or ignored it. His son was given a grand welcome before he even got off the train. There was so much fanfare, with bands playing and friends and family cheering and crowding the platform, that a bewildered Pujji left his baggage on the train as it pulled away.

Soon the finishing touches had been made to a traditional wedding which would see the reunited couple marry in style. There was just one departure from custom. Even now, Pujji was under orders to show his colours. "I was in uniform even for my marriage, because the forces said we had to be in uniform whenever outside the house – even for such a ceremony," recalls Pujji.

The special day in November 1944 was a proud one for the twenty-six-year-old Pujji, if a little embarrassing at times. He was surprisingly coy and modest, given his remarkable achievements. At the behest of his family, a self-conscious Pujji rode a stunningly beautiful white horse to the ceremony as the photographer buzzed around, trying to capture every possible moment and angle.

"I didn't want to ride the horse, but my sisters insisted. I loved my family and they were waiting for me for so many years that I wanted to do whatever they wanted me to do," said Pujji.

At Amrit's house in Ludhiana, the couple walked around the Sikh holy book four times and, with that, became man and wife. "It was a wonderful atmosphere because I had come back alive," said Pujji. "We then held a celebration in one of the best restaurants in New Delhi. There were many pictures in the newspapers of that party. It was a very happy occasion for everyone – for me, my family and friends. On this occasion we had the privilege to meet two notable personalities: Mahatma Gandhi and the legendary poet Rabindranath Tagore."

After the jubilation died down, the couple had a chance to be alone at last and enjoy their honeymoon. Pujji wanted nothing more than to go back to the stunning views and fresh air of Simla, his mountainous birthplace in the far north of India. They spent two weeks in a five-star hotel there.

For Pujji it was a wonderful chance both to get to know his wife – they had spent only a matter of weeks with each other – and to reflect on his life so far. Simla was familiar to him, but it was rooted in a distant memory of a very different life – a life before the war, a life as a refuelling superintendent looking for adventure. Simla had seen a young Pujji excel in sports on its streets and fields and begin to dream about flying. He now returned there as one of the most highly decorated pilots of the twentieth century.

Amrit was intrigued about his Simla childhood, and Pujji spent many happy days showing her where he was born and where he lived and played as a youth. For the first time in many years, Pujji completely relaxed.

Although Pujji's war was over, he was not out of the military. As soon as his honeymoon was over he returned to New Delhi, where he was told he must go to Quetta in what is now Pakistan, near its mountainous border with Afghanistan. A Dakota plane was waiting for him. It was December 1944.

He and his wife were greeted with a spacious, four-bedroomed house on the college grounds, and Pujji began the course. It might at first have seemed like a pleasant step down after years of dangerous operational duties, but Pujji found the six-month course difficult. It was a big change. Pujji was a pilot, but the college catered for all the armed forces and the course required a certain military discipline that was new to him. Suddenly, he had to learn rifle drill and spend time square-bashing like any raw army recruit. It had also been years since Pujji had been a student in the classroom. The last time had been as a would-be RAF pilot who had just arrived in England. Now every morning was crammed with lesson after lesson on military tactics, administration and organisation.

"For me it was more tough because I had not been in the army. I had never done parades. It was that side of things that I found hard. I had never done the 'left, right' or weapons drill. I still don't know how to hold a rifle," laughed Pujji.

But, in between the lessons and marching, he still found time to enjoy his new married life. For example, it was during a spare afternoon in the hilly city that he taught his wife how to ride a bicycle.

Their love grew and Pujji and his wife became inseparable. "I never accepted an invitation without her, and it was the same with her," he said. "It was an unwritten understanding that we would be together all the time. I was a very happy man because of that." It remained that way until her death forty-five years later in 1989.

As well as enjoying the healthy glow of a young marriage, Pujji was to experience another defining moment during his studies at the military college – one of recognition.

After several months of study, a telegram arrived for Pujji in April 1945 from the Government of India on behalf of Lord Mountbatten. It told him he had been awarded the Distinguished Flying Cross. This decoration, given to those officer pilots demonstrating exemplary gallantry in the face of the enemy, had come without warning or explanation.

"My wife kept asking me what the telegram said. I was very emotional and could not answer. She initially thought there was something wrong because I didn't say anything," remembers Pujji. "It just said congratulations. It was a wonderful surprise. It was the ultimate recognition of all my achievements."

It was at emotional times like this that Pujji would simply go into a room and close the door. In public, Pujji had always conducted himself as he thought a leader and figurehead should – showing little emotion and taking command of a situation. It was perhaps this stoic persona that helped him survive and thrive during four years of danger and personal loss. But, in private, he was a sensitive person, and he was affected by good news as much as the next man.

Pujji and Amrit were invited to a presentation and lunch with Lord Mountbatten at the Viceroy's House in New Delhi. It was a ceremony which Pujji equated to being honoured at Buckingham Palace. The last time he had seen Lord Mountbatten had been amid the danger and death of the Burmese jungle, although Pujji doubted if he would have remembered that.

Air Marshal Sir Keith Park later wrote to Pujji: 'This note is to convey my warmest congratulations on the award of your Distinguished Flying Cross. I am delighted that your gallant record has received this special recognition.'

The palace presentation came against the backdrop of the end of the Second World War. Pujji remembers being absolutely delighted at the news. His good fortune – and no small amount of skill – had seen him through the war. He had got married, received one of the highest military honours and been appointed a member of the Services Selection Board in Dehradun. He was to choose the leaders of the future for the army, navy and air force. Even now, sixty years later, Pujji can go to an armed-forces reunion and be warmly greeted by a retired general who will show his gratitude to Pujji for choosing him. Shaping the leadership of the forces was an important post carrying much responsibility.

On the home front there was more good news – Amrit was expecting a baby. Pujji was overjoyed. He was in a position where he could be proud of his past, present and future, but Pujji would not get a chance to settle into his post or see the birth of his child. He had one more battle to face.

CHAPTER SEVEN

A New Fight for Survival

In February 1946, aged just twenty-seven, Pujji was diagnosed with tuberculosis – a disease that was a regular killer in the post-war era. Pujji could not believe it. He had survived untold skirmishes and brushes with death in the skies only to be laid low by disease. He was later told that constant flying at high altitudes without adequate oxygen had probably left him vulnerable to TB.

He was sent straight to a military hospital in Poona, near Bombay. There he was examined and told the worst possible news – the infection had attacked both lungs.

"They said there's no treatment and I have only to wait for my death in six months to a year," remembers Pujji. Amrit was due to give birth in just one month's time. Pujji had held off marrying her in wartime so his beloved would not become a war widow. Doctors were now telling him she would become a TB widow instead.

By this point in his life, Pujji had lost his fear of death. Every day, both during and after the war, had been a bonus for him. But what he could not stand was being away from his family during his last months. He was stuck in Poona, many hundreds of miles away from his wife, his brothers and sisters and his parents in New Delhi.

"I wasn't scared. I always thought I was going to die while flying. I had told my parents not to expect me back. But I thought it would be a little more pleasant for me to die among my own people," said Pujji.

So he put in a request to be transferred to a hospital closer to home. His doctors refused because of the risk that he would spread the highly infectious disease.

This was too much for Pujji. He had not dedicated his life to fighting for others only to be told that he could not get a simple transfer to spend his final days near his loved ones. This decorated pilot felt he deserved this at least.

So, as his native India was on the verge of shaking off its colonial trappings and becoming an independent nation, he wrote to Lord Mountbatten, Viceroy of India. He made clear his final wish.

Soon it was arranged for him to take the long train journey to a hospital in Kasauli, near his hometown and family, and Pujji travelled in some style.

"They reserved a whole train carriage for me because I was very contagious," remembers Pujji. "It was for the disease, not for my comfort, but it was nice all the same. In those days it was a dreaded disease. I had two nurses caring for me."

Pujji had got his wish. He was soon being cared for in a palatial room at the hospital.

As the weeks and months ticked by towards his anticipated death, Pujji had time to dwell on how his wife and unborn child were faring. Although TB was expected to kill him, he still felt remarkably able.

"TB is a very strange disease. It's not like having a temperature. All you know is that you are going to die. You can walk around because, physically, you feel all right," he said.

While Pujji had been on his sickbed, Amrit had travelled back to her family home in Ludhiana to have the child.

Amrit brought a healthy baby girl into the world in March 1946. She was called Veena.

The months went by and Pujji grew impatient for progress – be it his own death or a chance to see his first, and probably his only, child. He was trapped in limbo, and the uncertainty and powerlessness he felt was terrible.

Although he was frustrated and tormented, Pujji was not one to sit back and let events take their course. If he decided something should happen, he would stop at nothing to make sure it did. He may have long since lost his fear of death, but he resolved to get better in order to see Amrit and Veena.

The months passed. Pujji was confined to the hospital, fighting to improve his strength. He was kept sane only by regular family visits, although never from those who were young or vulnerable to infections.

Pujji still cannot quite believe that he survived. The medical profession were clueless as to what brought him through, he remembers. "It was a miracle how I recovered," he said. "I put it down to the love and affection of my family – my wife, children and parents. They kept me happy. And cod liver oil helped too."

After nearly six months in hospital he was still sick but not contagious. To Pujji this meant only one thing: a chance to see Veena. However, the health authorities still wouldn't allow it; his plea to let her visit fell on deaf ears. Pujji could not write another letter to Lord Mountbatten on this matter, so a plot to smuggle the child into his room was hatched.

"We had to bring her secretly. The doctors had specifically said 'Don't bring your child.' But, in fact, my wife went on to bring her once a week. We did all the wrong things," admitted Pujji. As soon as he saw his child, now about four months old, the previous six months of struggle suddenly seemed worthwhile. It was the tonic he needed. "I was never too ill to enjoy being with Veena," he added.

He even gathered enough energy one day to steal out and enjoy a picnic with his young family. To Pujji's mind, it was relatives and friends that had helped him thus far, and they would see him through to a full recovery.

A restored Pujji eventually came home, having spent a year in hospital.

He had survived his traumatic ordeal, but Pujji's life was yet again to change fundamentally. The disease had seen him invalided out of the military. His career on the selection board was over and his time as an officer ended abruptly. He requested that they reinstate him, but he was told he had a 100% disability pension and that was that – no more flying with them.

The world around him was also changing. In 1947, India gained independence. Pujji, the civilian, now had to find a way to make a new career for himself and provide for his family in a brave new world.

Fortunately, Pujji had ideas and a new zest for life. He was offered a senior position back at Shell – the company he had left in order to go and fight the war, not expecting to come back alive. He took it, but soon a new offer came along. "Since I recovered I didn't want to sit in one place," he said. "And when India got independence the government asked what job I wanted. I said they can only give me a ground job. So they offered me the position of aerodrome officer, in charge of an airport. I accepted the offer and was posted to New Delhi."

Pujji began to learn the ropes and adjust to civilian life. He soon mastered the day-to-day running of the airport and became involved in every aspect, even becoming a qualified air traffic controller. There was no division of labour in those days. He had absolute control.

"I was in charge of operations and administration. Then I also trained as a flight control officer. I became responsible for everything – from landing planes and whatever was going on in the terminal building to where the taxis waited. It was a big job," remembers Pujji.

His post in New Delhi also meant he played a part in pivotal moments in his country's history. The following year Mahatma Gandhi's assassin was brought to the airport and Pujji was asked to lock him up for the night. Nathuram Godse had shot the iconic leader and then given himself up to police.

CHAPTER EIGHT

Racing Against the Odds

Pujji was then sent to Nagpur, in Maharashtra, in 1951 and to Dibrugarh, in Assam, in 1952. During this time, Pujji continued to break new ground. Despite being invalided out of the air force, he flew in India's 1st National Air Race. It took place in 1950 in Calcutta. It was a 350-mile circuit and was open to pilots from across the world. However, because it was the first one, it turned out to be a domestic affair, with about fifteen Indian pilots vying for the first title. Flying an L5 light aircraft, Pujji came second, winning the Nehru Trophy (the winner was awarded the President's Trophy).

"Everybody knew that my department had said I was unfit to fly," remembers Pujji, but his staff and colleagues were proud of his achievements and no one complained.

Some may say Pujji took part in the contest to satisfy a need for the exhilaration and danger that had become his staple diet during the war years, but Pujji said he simply loved flying, in all its forms.

"In the RAF I was flying fast and powerful aircraft, but in the L5 I was doing only eighty miles an hour. It wasn't the same. And there was no one trying to shoot at you. But I didn't miss the danger. I had put that behind me. I was happy doing what I was doing. I don't look back, and the future I don't bother with. I just want to be happy where I am. I'm very lucky that I have peace of mind," said Pujji.

The organisers of the race were certainly grateful for his

participation. In February 1951, the chairman of the Aero Club of India, Bajrang Bahadur Singh, wrote to Pujji: 'Whatever little success the rally has achieved is entirely due to the interest that you have taken.'

The first event was evidently judged worthy of a sequel, and so, a year later, the 2nd National Air Race took place. Neither the fact that he was theoretically an invalid nor the birth of his second child, Satinder, interrupted Pujji's ambition to win this time.

This race was on a grander scale and much more daunting. It was flown over three days on a gruelling 1,000-mile course, and the venue was Kanpur. The second event attracted international pilots, professional racers. Pujji was the only amateur flyer.

An air race may conjure up images of light aircraft zipping around a well-marked figure-of-eight course, pleasantly set within view of spectators. Those events would come later; the first races were long-distance. There was a take-off point, a landing point and a route. Pilots were expected to read maps, keep their bearings and plot their course, all while trying for the quickest possible time.

The first race was a warm-up, but soon it was time for the real thing, and there was no small amount of in-flight drama. Pujji had to battle with an aircraft damaged by flying debris and then he suffered the sudden loss of his maps.

"Something hit the window. I was holding the map at the time and it just flew out of the window. Fortunately, it was on the last stage," remembers Pujji. He went on to win the race. It was a wonderful moment for Pujji when he raised the President's Trophy. "Everybody said it was because of the joy of having my son that I won," said Pujji.

The victory was a sweet one, not just for Pujji but for many of his countrymen. His win had put India on the flying map. He was a champion among his compatriots, and his name appeared in all the newspapers – just as it had during the war years.

However, after two air races, Pujji received a letter stating that, because he had been invalided out of the air force, his pilot's licence

Invited by the Italian Government.

Laying a wreath.

Pujji leading the parade.

Pujji with the mayor and mayoress.

FLOWER PRINCESS MEETS PENSIONERS

DECORATED: Greeting for Diana from Mohinder Singh Pujji

Diana's a winner with old soldiers

PRINCESS Diana melted hearts when she braved the biting cold to visit old people yesterday.

Festooned with a garland of carnations, she delighted 300 members of an Asian day centre in Southall, West London, and dispelled any doubts that the Royal Family was doing its duty during the Gulf War.

Mangal Singh, 73, displaying a chest full of medals from his days fighting Rommel, said: "I think they all do a fine job."

The Princess was welcomed by former Squadron Leader Mohinder Singh Pujji who, as the first Indian to join the RAF in the Second World War, was Lord Mountbatten's personal pilot.

Princes Diana meets Pujji.

Pujji honoured by the French and Belgian governments.

Pujji with Prince Charles.

Pujji with the chief of the Indian Air Force, Nagina and Amarjit.

Pujji with the chief of the Indian Air Force, Nagina, Amarjit and Angela.

Pujji meets Princess Anne.

Pujji with Princess Anne and Lord Slim.

Pujji honoured by the Sikh community in London.

Pujji's acceptance speech.

Pujji and family at the award ceremony.

Honorary Aldermen and Honorary Freemen of the borough

From left to right (top row) Thomas James Duncan, Councillor Michael John Dudding, OBE TD DL, (bottom row) Squadron Leader Mohinder Singh Pujji, DFC RCS IM, IAF Marjorie Edith Hellps, MBE and Stanley Higgwood

'The Famous Five' of Newham.

Document making Pujji an honorary freeman of the Borough of Newham.

Pujji laying a wreath.

Newham party with family.

Dave Burbage
Chief Executive

Member Services
Chief Executive's Department

Newham Town Hall,
East Ham, London, E6 2RP
tel: 020-8430-2000 ext 21050
Direct Dial: 020-8430-3316
fax: 020-8472-3530
john.mattock@newham.gov.uk

Ask for: John Mattock
Your ref:
Our ref: COM/7RM
Date: 4 August, 2000

Squadron Leader M S Pujji, DFC

Dear Squadron Leader Pujji,

I am pleased to advise you that the Council, at a special meeting held on the 24 July, unanimously agreed to confer on you the Honorary Freedom of the London Borough of Newham in recognition of the distinguished public services rendered by you as a former serving officer in the RAF and to the community of the London Borough of Newham.

The Mayor's Advisory Sub-Committee has been authorised to determine the detailed arrangements for the ceremony to confer this award and at a meeting on Monday of this week considered a preliminary report on the arrangements. I am able to advise you that the ceremony will take place on the evening of the 12 October in the Large Hall at the Town Hall, East Ham, E6 and this will be followed by a reception.

Five people have been chosen to receive an award on this evening. In consultation with the Mayor and Council's Business Manager, I have been authorised to draw up the guest list. In this respect, as well as yourself and a personal guest, you are invited to put forward the names of twenty people who you would like to be invited.

A commemorative brochure will be produced and this will include a photograph and resume about each recipient of an award. In order to prepare the resume, it would be helpful if you could provide some information about your career and the work you have been involved with in the community, particularly any community activity in Newham. Please send this information to John Mattock at the above address. This will supplement information we already have within the Council. Once a draft has been prepared, I will forward a copy to you for your comments.

The Mayor's Advisory Sub-Committee will be meeting again in September to finalise the arrangements. However, if you have any questions about the award, the ceremony or the arrangements, please do not hesitate to contact John Mattock on 020 8430 3316.

Yours sincerely,

Dave Burbage
Chief Executive

The letter notifying Pujji that he had been granted the freedom of the Borough of Newham.

Pujji with the Mayor of Newham.

Pujji with Manju, Satish and Sharda.

Award from Gravesend Council.

Painting of Pujji's Aircraft by Russel.

Honour for the RAF hero who lived the high life

Above: Mohinder aged 82 and (left) as a young pilot at Biggin Hill.

When wartime Prime Minister Winston Churchill immortalised 'the Few' who defeated Germany's air armada in the Battle of Britain, he wasn't just recognising the English airmen who made up the majority of the RAF at that crucial time.

Volunteers from Britain's colonies and from countries already over-run by German forces played a crucial role in the victory, and in the years of war that remained ahead.

Among them was Mohinder Singh Pujji who volunteered in India and was based at Biggin Hill during the battle.

Now 82, Squadron Leader Pujji is a popular member of the Guru Nanak Day Centre in Gravesend and lives in a sheltered housing scheme opposite.

Just before this year's Remembrance Day, he was honoured with the Freedom and an Honorary Aldermanship of Newham where he used to live, and by Kent County Council.

Social Services Chairman Keith Ferrin said: "We all owe a great debt to people like Squadron Leader Pujji who fought so bravely for us. He is an inspiration to everyone who meets him."

Mohinder is able to relate stories of hair-raising dog-fights over Kent, being shot down in Egypt and fighting the Japanese in Burma, as well as a successful rescue mission of 350 stranded American troops which earned him the Distinguished Flying Cross.

After the war, he went home to India and developed a passion for gliding, numbering Prime Minister Nehru and Lady Mountbatten of Burma among his passengers. Over the years he met other celebrities including the Queen, Princess Diana and Jackie Kennedy.

He also won the last 2,000-mile Indian National Air Race in 1967, the World Gliding Championships in 1968 and an 1,800-mile car race the following year.

He went on to fly jumbo jets for Air India and ran Bombay Airport before moving back to Britain in 1974 to work as an air traffic controller at Heathrow.

Above: Escorting Jackie Kennedy, and (below) with Indian Prime Minister Nehru.

An article about Pujji published in 2001.

Pujji's eighty-fourth birthday party, in the USA.

Pujji's eighty-fourth birthday party, in the USA.

Pujji's eighty-fourth birthday party, in the USA.

Pujji's eighty-fourth birthday party, in the USA.

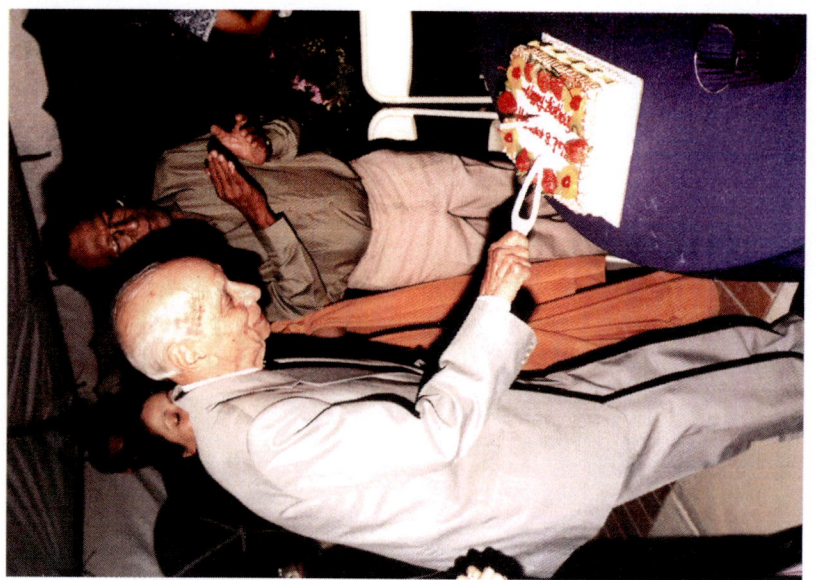

Pujji and family at his eighty-fourth birthday party.

had been withdrawn. For Pujji, this was like withdrawing access to the air he breathed. It also puzzled Pujji that the arrival of this letter came after he had been flying for six years and had even been given official permission to buy his own aircraft – an Aeronca.

So Pujji did what he always did when faced with an obstacle: he fought. Pujji began to pile on the pressure to have his licence reinstated. Eventually, a joint military and civilian board of experts was convened to decide whether he was capable of flying. A raft of medical tests and interviews later, they still could not make a decision.

This was an infuriating time for Pujji. He felt as though his life was in limbo. He had flown all over the world and dazzled many with his skills. Now he managed a busy airport and had never been so close to so many different kinds of aeroplanes, yet he could not take to the air. A more perfect kind of torment could not have been chosen for him. And it dragged on for years.

He persevered and pressed the panel of experts to consider what they were taking away from him. He simply did not stop.

"They said it was in my own interest to stop flying," said Pujji; "but I said, 'If you reject me, I will not survive.' They laughed at me. Then they agreed, on condition that I give up my disability pension. I was happy with that. Money has never been a great attraction to me."

The wheels had moved slowly, but ultimately the board found in Pujji's favour. In 1954, after countless wrangles, he was once again free to fly with a clear conscience. The next international air race was now firmly in his sights.

It was held in 1962. The course was spread over 1,500 miles from Jaipur to Madras, as it was then known. Again, he was surrounded by about twenty professional pilots and instructors. He was again the only amateur – a busy manager who grabbed a few hours of flying time whenever work and family commitments allowed. He was the only pilot to fly the first Indian-built aeroplane, called the Pushpak.

"I was the only person not flying for money. They practised

day and night, whereas I only flew in races and I had to pay for my flying. I only flew if someone wanted a joyride," said Pujji.

Pujji won that race too, with the most senior flight instructor in India coming second. As he raised the trophy, Pujji became a hero once again. Even the Prime Minister sent his congratulations.

Below is an account Pujji wrote shortly after the Air Race:

> I landed at Madras on the 26th January 1962 and since the race was to start on the 29th, I decided to go over the course. I had not been to any of these airfields before, and I thought it might save time in locating these when the race was on. I set forth on my familiarisation trip on the afternoon of 26th. I did not care to follow the route which was set by the authorities, I took short-cuts. I landed at Bangalore on 27th. Early next morning I took off for Coimbatore and reached there in two hours whereas in the race I took an hour and forty minutes. From Coimbatore to Trivandrum it took another two hours and thirty five minutes. The weather at Trivandrum was fairly bad, and I was advised not to fly that afternoon. Since I had very little time at my disposal, I did not want to risk reaching Madras late. I therefore took off from Trivandrum and set my course for Madurai right across the Western Ghats. As I flew across, I found myself in a valley with very high hills around me which were covered with thick clouds. I did not know what to do, my aircraft was not suitable for instrument flying and I therefore could not enter the clouds, and without entering the clouds, I just could not go over the hills. Finding myself in a tight corner, I had to make very steep turns, it was a miracle that somehow I managed to clear the hills. I think that I must have lost at least a pint of blood.
>
> I heaved a sigh of relief when I sighted Trivandrum. I then set my course again to Maduri but this time via Cape Comorin.
>
> I reached Maduri at 1545 hrs and I took off from there at 1620 hrs. I landed at Trichy after an hour and ten minutes. It had already become dark by then, and I decided to spend the night at Trichy. On the morning of 28th I took off from Trichy at 0620 hrs and landed at Madras at 0845 hrs reaching there, I contacted the Aero

Club authorities and after confirming that I could report to them by the evening, I decided to make a trip to Cuddappa and back, it took me three hours and forty.

I had thus covered all the airfields, except Cochin, Hyderabad and Bellary.

I was fortunate enough to win the race beating the Chief Flying Instructors of the Madras Flying Club (sponsors). My familiarisation flights certainly helped me to save time in locating different airfields, as well as warning me of the dangers to be encountered over the Western Ghats.

On the 29th January the big event took place and I was presented The President Trophy by the Prime Minister of India.

Pujji would fly in one last race, in 1967. It was a 2,000-mile course this time, from Bombay to Trivandrum in Southern India. This time there were so many pilots wanting to enter that organisers had to hold a special selection stage halfway through the race. Only the top eight were allowed to compete in the final stages.

When Pujji won the contest he became a national hero. India had held four international air races and Pujji had won three of them.

"It was a miracle. I didn't expect it. When I reached Southern India, everyone lifted me on their shoulders. They were so happy. I'm from Northern India, and they don't like people from there very much, so it was very surprising. The same trophy I had returned after the previous victory I now got to keep," said Pujji.

He also became an icon of the Indian aviation industry, which was still in its infancy. The Pushpak, built by India, which Pujji flew in the last two races, had previously been deemed unreliable by many. But it had now become a race-winner, the best evidence of its capabilities. The manufacturers were so grateful they wrote him a personal letter of thanks.

But one communication he received made him laugh. It was from the Government of India and it marked a distinct change of attitude towards him and his flying.

"I had requested more time off to go to the final air race, but, as a civil servant, I was told the Government of India had decided it couldn't give me paid leave. It would not pay me and would accept no liability if I crashed. But when I won I received a telegram congratulating me on my successes." said Pujji.

General K. M. Cariappa, the army's chief of staff, also conveyed his thanks. 'I hope it will encourage the youth of our country to be more air-minded,' he wrote.

However, as well as drawing much admiration, Pujji was ruffling a few feathers and perhaps denting a few egos. Many could not fathom how this part-timer could come along and repeatedly steal the limelight.

"Everybody in aviation knew me by this time. I heard people saying, 'We don't understand, how he does it?' But even I don't know. I would get telegrams about it from all over. I have at least 100 of those kinds of telegrams still in my files," said Pujji.

During his ascent to racing stardom, Pujji had found it ever more difficult to pay for his flying – it was now a privilege rather than part of his job. He also had to support his family. After securing his pilot's licence he still took his wife and two children up into the sky for pleasure trips, but this was becoming ever more rare. By 1954, Pujji had returned to his cherished New Delhi airport – except this time it was to the international airport. It was a position of some standing. For the second time in his life, he had reached the top of his profession. He would stay in the post there for another six years.

His status meant he was often invited to important state functions at stately properties that had their own landing strip. It was not unusual for the guests to fly in and out, but Pujji had to start thinking about other ways of getting his flying fix. This became even more of a pressing matter after the birth of his third child, Rita.

So, in 1956, Pujji took up gliding at Delhi Flying Club. His new hobby presented a whole new, terrifyingly engineless challenge for the thirty-eight-year-old to get his teeth into.

Somewhat predictably, he soon picked it up and became honorary chief gliding instructor. It was a far cry from the roar of the warplanes he had torn around in above three different continents. "Gliding is a wonderful, relaxing sport. You are flying just like a bird. It's the lack of noise that makes it soothing. On a plane there's always so much racket," remembers Pujji.

For him, gliding was much better than powered flight for pure enjoyment. "It depends on your purpose," he said. "Gliding is just a pleasure, but flying you can use for other purposes. When I was doing both I preferred gliding because it felt like you were going up into heaven."

These exact sentiments were shared by Pandit Nehru, the first prime minister of the newly independent India, when Pujji was given the privilege of taking him for a spin. The two often met, given Pujji's tendency to rise to the top in any field of achievement he turned his hand to. He later showed the joy of climbing into the skies to other members of the powerful Nehru dynasty, including Indira Gandhi's two sons, who were Nehru's grandsons.

"When I took up Prime Minister Nehru the first time he was thrilled," remembers Pujji. "He said, 'Pujji, I feel I'm in heaven.' There was no disturbance. He could talk to me because there was no noise. I showed him his palace from above for fifteen to twenty minutes."

Perhaps Nehru's calm reaction showed the mettle of a man used to a challenge; even pilots themselves did not always adjust well to the concept of flying without an engine.

Pujji remembers once taking a British Airways captain for a gliding excursion – one which held a few surprises for the poor pilot.

"The captain said to me, 'Gliding must be very thrilling; would you fly me?' I said yes. I took him up. It was an almost vertical take-off. We were pulled by a winch on a steel rope. He later said, 'I have been flying for twenty years and I have never felt more scared than when you took off.' Once he was up he was happy."

Pujji also met US President Dwight D. Eisenhower and offered to fly him in a glider. He, however, asked Pujji to take his naval aide instead. 'I have always been grateful to you for my first, and unfortunately last, glider flight. I recall it very well,' wrote E. P. Aurand years later from his rear-admiral's office in the Pentagon.

But taking VIPs for pleasure flights and enjoying a few barrel rolls in the sky could only sate Pujji for so long. He needed another challenge, which is why in 1960 he attempted to become the first Indian glider pilot to gain the Gold C.

The Gold C is a badge and benchmark of gliding skill. To earn one, a pilot has to gain a height of 3,000 metres or more, travel a distance of at least 300 kilometres and stay in the air for five hours or more – although not necessarily all on the same flight.

Pujji passed with flying colours during a trip from his base in New Delhi, and he was awarded the badge by the Fédération Aéronautique Internationale in Paris. His achievement made the headlines in the *Hindustan Times*, but other papers covered it in a rather unusual way.

"When I did the Gold C, I landed in a field because there was no aerodrome. All the villagers gathered round, and in newspapers the next day they said an aeroplane crash-landed but luckily the pilot was safe. They didn't realise it was a glider," recalls Pujji.

British magazine *Sailplane & Gliding* wrote to congratulate him on his achievement, requesting a written account of the challenge. People in Britain are 'always interested to hear what Indian thermals are like, as we assume they are much better than the thermals we get in this country', wrote editor Alan Slater.

Six years later, Pujji attempted the Diamond C – the pinnacle of gliding achievement. This involved gaining at least 5,000 metres in height, flying at least 500 kilometres and completing a separate 'goal' flight (in which you nominate your destination beforehand) covering a distance of at least 300 kilometres. This kind of undertaking required an area where he could take advantage of plenty of rising air currents – so Pujji chose Indian mountain range the Western Ghats for his goal flight. He became the first glider pilot to try such a daring feat there.

The expertise gained through regular weekend trips of more than 240 kilometres paid off – and possibly saved his life.

"This was a real challenge. In normal gliding you fly around everywhere – anybody can do it. But when you make a declaration of your planned destination before you go up, it becomes a very different thing. In this case, it was a question of life and death. There was no place to land, and sometimes there were no thermals. If you come down in the hills, you are finished," said Pujji.

Despite looming bad weather, Pujji pulled it off.

"I took about six hours," he added. "It was worrying at times, when I thought I wasn't going to make it. There's nothing you can do except pray. Of course skill comes into play. However, if you become nervous and lose your heart, then the chances are you will fail."

The following is an account Pujji wrote shortly after the experience:

> *I applied for two days casual leave to go to Poona and attempt a cross-country flight in a glider. On 15th April 1966 I made the successful flight. A detailed account of my flight is given hereunder:*

It was a doubtful day with patches of stratus clouds here and there. I got my first launch at 1130 hrs which gave me no lift and I landed back immediately afterwards. I was launched a second time at 1150 hrs and was released at an initial height of 1,000ft. While coming down in the circuit I got a weak lift at 500ft. After a struggle of about 30 minutes I climbed up to 3,000ft. The time was then approx. 1230 hrs and I had to immediately take a decision whether to make the attempt on this day or not. It was to be now or never; considering the various other factors like the necessity for me to return to Bombay International Airport by Sunday to relieve my No. 2 going on leave, and also the consideration that other members of the club had also to make an attempt, I decided to set forth.

My ultimate destination was Belgaum – a distance of 305km. If I were in an aeroplane the course to steer was 155°. However, I was to keep strictly to the road to facilitate easy and early retrieve. The passage of the road was not straight in this hilly area and the circuitous route meant at least another 50km.

I crossed the first ridge of hills at a height of 3,000ft that I had gained over my base, Poona Gliding Centre. I had hoped that after crossing this ridge I would have the initial advantage of this height to go forward and look for more thermals; but to my disappointment I found myself over a plateau with only 500ft or so to spare. I could not possibly think of continuing my flight at this low altitude and as I went along the road, I started looking for a field where I could land. This was an area of 'no sink' and I gained another 100ft while I followed the road to the small village of Saswad. I had half a mind to land here and send a quick message to Poona to retrieve me; but then I decided to take advantage of whatever little height I had gained and land further along the road, thus adding a few more kilometres to my distance if possible.

As I glided along the road, losing very little height, I saw that the road further ahead passed through two lofty hill-tops and disappeared.

There was a steep fall of hundreds of feet. The space between the hill-tops was not very wide and it was difficult to make even a circuit therein. My height here was only 200ft above ground level and I had either to go in for a straight landing on a field or to follow the road and glide into the unknown. I was not very sure of reaching the end and therefore left the decision to fate, i.e., if I did not reach I would land beside the road and if I did, I did not know what would happen.

I skimmed over and cleared the edge with the minimum speed and dived into the depth. I did this to gain speed, so that I could manoeuvre my Glider to get out of strong down currents, if any. Fortunately I found strong up currents instead at this spot and immediately started circling. Before I could recover from the shock of the extraordinary action that I had taken in plunging into the unknown, I found I was gaining height rapidly and within 15 minutes I had reached an altitude of 8,000ft. Feeling quite happy, I then once again set forth towards my goal. The sky was becoming over cast but the gain in height enabled me to proceed at good speed. I was mostly in 'no sink' areas, I did not find many thermals, but there were no down currents either. I reached Kolhapur (almost half the total distance) at about 1500 hrs but my height had reduced to 4,000ft. As I proceeded south, I continued to make good progress but I did not gain much height.

I was now flying on the fringe of Western Ghats and my height above ground was not very much more than a few hundred feet. My destination was still approximately 70km away, and there appeared no possibility my being able to reach my goal. Therefore once again I started looking for a place to land. To my dismay I found that there was no level ground around. The hills were steep. There was no space on the sides of the main road and the road itself was neither wide enough nor straight for me to attempt a landing. The whole area was rocky and uneven. I realised that I did not have any chance of a safe landing anywhere in this area and my efforts were then diverted to make a crash landing somewhere where I could find any habitation. This I thought would be useful if I survived the landing. While these thoughts were going on in my mind I continued to go down the slopes.

Every circuit of mine was not more than 200 to 300ft above ground level. My eyes were eagerly looking for some sort of a place where I would eventually put the Glider down. I felt that my Glider hit a 'lift' area; I immediately started circling, making every effort to remain in the centre of this very weak thermal. My Veriometer read +1 but I continued undeterred and when I had made about a hundred or so steep circles and felt giddy, I noticed that I had gone up a little; from the corner of my eye I quickly glanced at the altimeter and read that I had gained 200 hundred feet. Now my Veriometer started registering increased lift. Gradually my height increased and so did the rate of my ascent. Soon I found that I was getting a lift of 10ft per second and soon I was at 10,000ft over the very spot where I was about to put the Glider down barely 25 minutes earlier. I could not believe that I had achieved this success. It was more of a miracle and I do not claim any credit for it. I then headed for Belgaum Airport once again; where I reached at 1630 hrs still having a height of 8000ft. Encouraged by the extraordinary luck, I decided to continue the flight and make an attempt to cover a record distance. I had 2 hrs of daylight left and with no sink I could easily have covered another 200km. I had gone 50km, without having lost any height whatsoever, when I found my path of flight blocked by a huge C.B. cloud (thunder storm). Undeterred and being in a buoyant and optimistic mood, I entered the dark clouds. Soon I found myself being tossed around violently. The weather was extremely turbulent and it was raining heavily. I could hear the thunder and there were flashes of lightning. I thought my Glider would break if I did not immediately get out of this. I did not consider it advisable to take the risk, and I turned around heading straight once again for my destination.

I reached Belgaum at 1730 hrs and flew over the Airport. I had not lost any height during the last one hour, even though I had covered a distance of approximately 100km. I saw an Indian Airlines Dakota on the side of the runway with passengers ready to board the service. I made a steep descent with spoilers (air brakes) out in my anxiety to land before the IAC Service took off for Bombay. I was now feeling very tired and worn out and was anxious to catch this service, to get back to Bombay.

I landed in the centre of the Airport on the runway itself at 1742 hrs, and rolled on to the site where the IAC Dakota was parked.

To achieve this final cherished pin on his lapel, Pujji had used a secret advantage: he had learned from the very best glider pilots in the world. They hailed from the nation he had spent several tours fighting against in Europe and Western Africa during the Second World War – the Germans.

CHAPTER NINE

Forgetting the Past – Paying a Visit to Post-War Germany

After the First World War, German pilots were not allowed to fly planes, so, in a move that Pujji would probably have secretly admired, they learned to glide instead. "There it's almost a religion. It's considered very spiritual," added Pujji.

The opportunity to learn did not come by design but by a chance encounter. Hanna Reitsch was Nazi Germany's first female test pilot. A civilian but a committed Nazi, she flew early versions of the V1 rocket bomb. It was her gliding experience that kept her from the dismal fate of many pilots attempting to help the war effort by guiding the flying bomb. In 1960, she paid a visit to India and Pujji met her.

Despite the huge gulf in wartime ideology (Hanna had also helped the Germans design the very planes Pujji fought against), they had an extraordinary set of meetings and became fast friends.

The first topic of conversation is easy to guess. "We talked a lot about the war," remembers Pujji. "She made no secret of helping her country, but she said she was a civilian and it was only because of her love for flying and adventure that she was doing the work. She didn't realise just how much damage she was doing to us. She never thought of it, she said."

A reciprocal invitation to Germany swiftly followed, and, the same year, Pujji led a group of five gliding instructors there to see how they conducted their flight training. Correspondence shows the six were to be treated as 'state guests' during a stay of almost three months. Between visits to gliding schools and a course to qualify as an advanced gliding instructor, there were evenings at the opera house, receptions held by the senate, and press conferences. From Frankfurt to Stuttgart, Wiesbaden to Freiburg and Munich to Bonn, Pujji and his colleagues enjoyed every privilege, accompanied by Hanna Reitsch.

"It was fun. Hanna had a great respect for me because of my flying-and-gliding record. We visited all the gliding centres. I was there for three months and she was my constant companion," said Pujji.

But there was no special treatment when Pujji requested they take part in the next instructor training course – they had to earn their pass certificate.

In an interim report dated 23 May 1960 – three weeks into his stay – Pujji wrote:

> Then followed extensive training including ground lectures. There were ten other German pilots in this course. We were also required to undergo a medical examination.
>
> At the end of the course, we were examined in theory (six-hour written paper) followed by flying tests. Each one of us had to make five examination flights with an inspector especially deputed by the government for the purpose. The result of the examination has not yet been communicated to us.

The challenge was made even harder by the fact that lectures were delivered in German, but Hanna Reitsch interpreted every word for them. 'It meant double work for all of us, but much more for her. It would not be wrong to say that, but for her, we would simply not have been able to go through this course,' Pujji added in his report.

And so, fifteen years after the Second World War ended, Pujji was given his official German glider pilot and instructor certificate, helping to build a valuable post-war relationship between the two countries.

Pujji took full advantage of the expert tuition he had received.

Aged fifty, he was awarded the opportunity to represent India at the 1968 World Gliding Championships in Warsaw, Poland. The acting Ambassador of Poland was at that time Pujji's childhood friend Mohinder Singh. It was a happy reunion.

Upon his return to India, Pujji was posted to Jaipur from New Delhi. His life as an aerodrome officer was one of constant change. He would rarely stay in any one place for more than three years. Given Pujji's desire for new challenges, it suited him well. He moved into his government-appointed four-bedroom bungalow without fuss and was this time given control of all the airports in Rajasthan. It was a massive undertaking.

Jaipur, the capital of Rajasthan, was a marvellous place, packed with ancient architecture and culture. It felt provincial compared with the hustle and bustle of New Delhi, but it had a beauty all its own, felt Pujji. The Pink City, with its slightly red-tinged sandstone buildings glowing bright, immediately impressed Pujji and his family.

And the city presented him with a blank canvas – gliding here was totally unheard of. Despite a huge workload in his day job, Pujji immediately set about finding a way to set up a gliding club. Help came from an unlikely source.

Banasthali Vidyapith was a special boarding school reserved for the daughters of the rich and famous. "They did horse riding – everything. In fact, the only thing they didn't do was flying and gliding. They accepted my suggestion and they opened a gliding-and-flying club under my control," said Pujji. The master aviator had touched on a way to leave a legacy that would inspire a new generation of pilots.

The next generation was certainly in Pujji's mind in 1962 when his eldest daughter, Veena, married Prem Gupta in Jaipur. "I was very happy," said Pujji. "And I was very lucky because the Maharajah gave me all the facilities I needed. He held a reception in the palace and attended the marriage with his wife."

Rubbing shoulders with great historical figures was becoming a regular feature of Pujji's life. Five years earlier, in 1957, he had met a true aviation hero and one of the most decorated pilots in history – winner of the Victoria Cross, Group Captain Sir Leonard Cheshire. One day he turned up on Pujji's doorstep in New Delhi. "He asked if I could fly him to Dehradun because there was no air service and he had some work to do," remembers Pujji. This was Pujji's chance to fly for one of the few people he looked up to. He wanted to impress the distinguished British pilot, who accompanied the pivotal mission to drop the atom bomb on Nagasaki. But, as it turned out, Pujji had to choose discretion over valour.

"I took him up in a Tiger Moth, as that was all we had – two-seater, one in front and one in the back. I made him sit in the front seat as my passenger," said Pujji. "We took off. After about an hour's flight there were hills about 8,000 feet high so we had to be careful. Suddenly, there were clouds appearing, which we entered. After a while Sir Leonard said, 'Pujji, are you sure you are going to get there, because the clouds are here and the hills are coming.' I asked him if he wanted to turn back, and in the end we did. He said thank you for the flight, even though we never made it. It was still an honour for me."

The flying legend later wrote a letter telling Pujji how much the experience had thrilled him. 'It was bad luck wasn't it?' Sir Leonard wrote. 'But nonetheless I really enjoyed it, and for some reason or another didn't seem to mind when we had to turn back. We did our best, didn't we?'

Later, in Jaipur in 1961, Pujji met the Queen and the Duke of Edinburgh when they came to visit, and, the following year, he entertained Jackie Kennedy, wife of the US president, showing her the city sights. He even had the opportunity to meet Soviet leader Leonid Brezhnev and Jovanka Broz, the wife of Yugoslavian leader Josip Tito.

But if life in Jaipur seemed hectic for a forty-six-year-old Pujji in 1964, nothing would prepare him for his next assignment – Bombay.

"That was a big change. It was the biggest airport in India

with hundreds of planes needing refuelling. It was as big as Heathrow," said Pujji. "I had twenty assistant officers under me, working around the clock. There always had to be someone on duty." In a 1967 article for the *Times of India*, Pujji told a reporter, "I am answerable for everything relating to the airport – from an air crash to the cleanliness of the toilets."

Nevertheless, Pujji flourished. "For me, the move was a pleasure. I was at a big airfield doing bigger jobs and meeting more VIPs. There were too many VIPs to count: the King of Nepal, presidents of India and the Aga Khan. Even film stars would come and chat with me. In Jaipur, people like that wouldn't come so much," he added.

And there were other perks that appealed to him. "I had a wonderful office on top of a three-storey building. On the top floor there was only my office," remembers Pujji.

But there were also solemn duties to perform. Not all the leading lights he was responsible for were living. He saw off Prime Minister Shastri on a flight to Moscow for a meeting there in 1966. A week later, it was one of Pujji's duties at the airport to receive and take charge of his coffin upon its return.

Bombay proved both the pinnacle and swansong for Pujji in his career as an aerodrome officer. After many years controlling airports across the country and breaking boundaries – including training the first two female Indian pilots – he itched to become more closely involved with flying the aircraft rather than worrying about where and how they landed and whether there were enough taxis for passengers. He felt as though he was working on the wrong side of the fence, constantly looking over. As he watched aircraft taking off, he felt that he was missing the real fun.

He began to look elsewhere, and he settled on a post as an operations superintendent for Air India, representing and supervising its jet pilots.

"It was my love for flying that was behind the move. As an aerodrome officer I would only fly for pleasure. Here I could fly as a supervisor of other pilots. And I attended pilot meetings all over the world, from New York to Manila," said Pujji.

But the move was not easy. The government refused to let Pujji work for Air India. The reason they gave was that he was required to take charge of Calcutta International Airport. "I felt that was just bloody-mindedness," remembers Pujji. "The senior officers in the department were jealous. They could see that I was flying most of the time and that it was what I always wanted. In my new job I flew Boeing 707s and attended meetings in all parts of the world. I had always asked for a job like this. So I declined their offer."

Pujji stuck to his guns, and by 1968 the move was a done deal. However, the day before he was due to leave, another spanner – or perhaps that should read *a bull* – was thrown in the works.

"An Air India Boeing took off in the middle of the night as a bull walked on the runway. This aircraft hit it but still went up," remembers Pujji. "When the pilot went to put his wheels up, he couldn't. He knew there was something wrong. He couldn't land because he had too much fuel; the runway wasn't long enough. I was woken up and I immediately came to the control tower. The pilot said, 'I don't know what it is, but I can't put my wheels up.' He wasn't sure if the wheels were damaged. He had 350 people on board. I told him to reduce his fuel and we would get fire crews ready for a landing. We called the city fire brigade as well as the airport brigade. It was my last day of work before getting the new job for Air India."

Fortunately the pilot managed to land safely. Pujji later found the bull's head – horns and all – stuck in the undercarriage. It was a miracle the incident hadn't turned into a major disaster. "I told the pilot we must not have publicity for this," added Pujji. "People will say, 'What was a bull doing on the runway?' But it was such a big incident everyone knew about it the next day anyway."

So Pujji successfully moved to his new post. Throughout the two years he was there, he had a wonderful time, speaking to pilots and getting to shadow them as they flew jets all over the

Pujji presented with a plaque on his eighty-fourth birthday.

Pujji presenting a picture to Prince Philip on behalf of Commonwealth veterans.

Pujji at his reception by the Queen.

Pujji talking to the Queen.

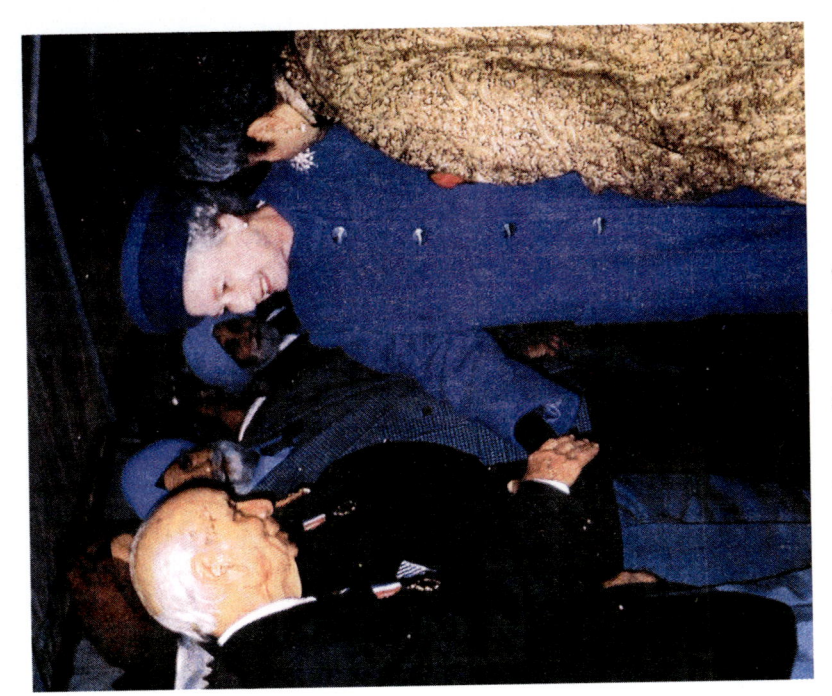

Pujji with his nephew Annu.

Pujji with Elsie.

An extract from an article published in the 2003 issue of the
BURMA STAR MAGAZINE

Edited by Squadron Leader Adrian Burns
Deputy Personnel Staff Officer to the
COMMANDER-IN-CHIEF
Headquarters Strike Command
ROYAL AIR FORCE

'THE INDIAN AIR FORCE IN BURMA
AND
WING COMMANDER MAHINDER PUJJI'

The achievements of the IAF in the Burma campaign
and elsewhere are remarkable'.

Mahinder Pujji was first commissioned as a Pilot Officer in the IAF Volunteer Reserve on 1st August 1940; Seconded to the RAF and immediately sent to London. He was posted to No.1 RAF Depot at Uxbridge on 8 October 1940, pending RAF conversion.

He completed the course and was awarded 'RAF Wings' on 16 April 1941.

Pujji joined No 43 RAF Fighter squadron (Hurricanes) at Drem Scotland on 2 June 1841, and then to No 258 (also hurricanes) at Kenley (south of London) on 26 June 1941.for active operational duty.

During all this time he flew operational sorties over occupied France and in defence of the UK. He was then posted to Air Headquarters, Western Desert Middle East.

The RAF recognises Pujji's contribution.

Pujji at a reception by DAV College, Amritsar.

Pujji and Veena at a reception by DAV College, Amritsar.

Pujji as chairman of the Undivided Indian Ex-Services Association.

Pujji on a dais with Prince Philip.

Pujji with Lord Slim at the reunion.

Commodore G H Edwardes OBE RN
WWII 60th Anniversary
Commemoration Team
Project Manager
Ministry of Defence

Mr Mahindra Pujji DFC
c/o UIESA
Southall Day Centre
20 Western Road
Southall
Middx
UB2 5DS

4th March 2005

Dear *Mr Pujji DFC & Mrs Pujji*

I am delighted to inform you that you, and your guest, have been invited to attend the Commemorative lunch at Buckingham Palace in the presence of Her Majesty the Queen.

The Palace are making arrangements to issue invitations to all attendees and they will write to you nearer the time giving further details. To that end, please complete the enclosed questionnaire and return it in the envelope provided by 18th March 2005, even though you may not wish to attend.

Commodore G H Edwardes OBE RN

An invitation to Buckingham Palace for Pujji and Satinder.

Group photograph. Pujji is standing behind Prince Philip and Lord Slim.

Flowers from the MOD.

Meenakshi and Shiv.

Pujji signing autographs.

154

Pujji with defence minister John Reed.

Pujji with Lady Slim.

Pujji with Nagina.

Mahinder Singh Pujji (1918-

Photos courtesy of Mahinder Singh Pujji

Mahinder Singh Pujji, who has lived in Gravesend for many years, was a fighter pilot during the Second World War. He flew a Hurricane and was based at airfields throughout SE England including RAF Manston. He was among many Indian pilots who joined the RAF around the time of the Battle of Britain and who helped resist the invasion of Britain by German forces. He also fought abroad and on one occasion located a lost troop of 300 American soldiers in the Burmese jungle. He saved their lives. Mahinder Singh Pujji became one of the few Asian pilots to be awarded the Distinguished Flying Cross.

Exploring Kent's cultural heritage.

Pujji invited to Singapore, with his family.

Pujji invited to Singapore, with his son.

The mayor of Brighton with members of Pujji's family.

Pujji with a Spitfire.

159

Pujji accepts an award from Kent Council.

Veena and Pujji meet the IAF chief.

SPECIAL REPORT

'What he has done, most people only dream of'

by Karen Jeal

FORMER Second World War pilot Mahinder Singh Pujji has been honoured twice in one week.

He received a standing ovation at a surprise presentation in Gravesend to mark his colourful and courageous career.

Despite his advancing years, the 89-year-old stood proudly to attention as Kent Police area commander Chief Superintendent Gary Beautridge paid tribute to the Sikh RAF squadron leader who was shot down twice while engaged in dog fights with German pilots.

Mr Pujji, of The Grove, Gravesend, was handed the special police award at a Civic Centre event to celebrate Black History Month (BHM) last Friday.

It was the second occasion in a week in which Mr Pujji was honoured.

Kent County Council presented Mr Pujji with a Black and Minority Ethnic Achievement Award just days before at a County Hall service.

Mr Pujji, who was awarded the Distinguished Flying Cross for saving 300 American soldiers surrounded by Japanese troops in the Burmese jungle, is one of only two surviving Indian fighter pilots who fought at the time of the Battle of Britain during 1940-42.

He is also the only Sikh fighter pilot who flew throughout the war without removing his turban - and even kept a spare in the cockpit in case he was shot down over enemy territory.

On receiving his latest award, Mr Pujji said: "I am proud the police have awarded me.

"I have never been aware I'm a black man. I was in the Air Force flying with British, American, Polish and Czech pilots and we were one community."

Ch Supt Beautridge said: "It's indicative of how closely this community works together that we can come and celebrate events like this.

"We are celebrating achievements and notably unique, brave, committed and dedicated people like Mr Pujji.

"He is a beacon, what he has done most people only dream of, but latterly he has devoted his life to public services."

Mr Pujji has accomplished many things in his long life, including being a basketball player, winning international air races, being a gliding medallist, jumbo jet pilot, air traffic controller at Heathrow, and manager at the International Strand Hotel.

He was in the police force for 10 years as an interpreter and advisor. He is well known to the Royal family and was even appointed to escort the then Lady Diana Spencer for the day as way of introduction to her royal duties

Mr Pujji, however, is modest about his admirers. He said: "I'm grateful people recognise my contribution because it's important, but I shouldn't be winning these awards, I haven't done anything."

Left and below, Mahinder Singh Pujji during his service as a RAF fighter pilot; right, with the Queen

Life in the air
Factfile on Mahinder Singh Pujji's aviation career

1918	Born in Simla, India
1936	Learned to fly at the Delhi Flying School, joined the RAF at Uxbridge and fought in Battle of Britain
1943	Fought in Middle East at Tobruk
1943	Fought the Japanese in Far East until 1945
1945	Awarded Distinguished Flying Cross; one of the highest military honours
1946	Aerodrome officer in Bombay; flew and worked with Air India until 1947
1960	Finished second in the Indian national air races
1960	Won the Indian air races over a distance of 1,450 miles
1967	Won Indian air races over 2,000 miles
1968	Won world gliding championship
1972	Retired from Air India and settled in Britain with family
1974	Became air traffic controller
1982	Finally retired from aviation

■ Three other Gravesham residents were recognised for their outstanding contribution to Kent life at the BME Achievement Awards at County Hall, Maidstone.

Claudette Brambie
BORN in Montserrat in the Caribbean, Claudette moved to Gravesend in 1968, aged 13.

She became a lynchpin for the Gravesend West Indian population, forming the Gravesend West Indian Association in 1982.

Her roles in the community included teaching at Church Street School in Gravesend, secretary and chair of the Gravesend West Indian Association football team, member of the Police Liaison Committee, and committee member for the Community Relations Association and Gravesham Churches Housing Association.

Poetry winners
BLACK has many different colours, what does it mean to you? This was the theme for a poetry competition held as part of Black History Month (BHM).

The winners were:
■ Under 10 - Mary Phillips
■ Ten to 13 - Shanice Evans.
■ Fourteen to 17 - Louise Ogunnaike
■ Over 18 - Angela Mills.

Farida Usman
FARIDA USMAN and her family moved to Gravesend in 1969. She took up voluntary work teaching Urdu. Her work led to the formation of a Muslim Women's Group in Gravesend and Dartford.

Gurbakhsh Singh Sivia
GURBAKHSH SINGH SIVIA, 75, moved to Gravesend in 1969, and taught at Southfields High School. He helped to produce children's booklets on the Sikh faith.

He has raised funds for UK and Indian charities, and has personally raised £326,000 for a home for the elderly, infirm and disabled in India.

Kent County Council saw her potential and took her on as a home and school liaison co-ordinator, assisting children whose first language is not English to raise their achievement levels at school.

Celebrate all year
THE main message to emerge from BHM is there is only one race – the human race. Everyone is equal.

Ron Hampton, chairman of the National Black Police Association in America told how BHM is just as important there as it is here, adding: "Black History Month started in here in 1976. We celebrate it in February, but we should celebrate Black History Month 12 months a year, it makes good sense."

Pujji's contribution during the Second World War is recognised.

Pujji is presented with a trophy by the IAF chief.

162

Pujji with his grandchildren.

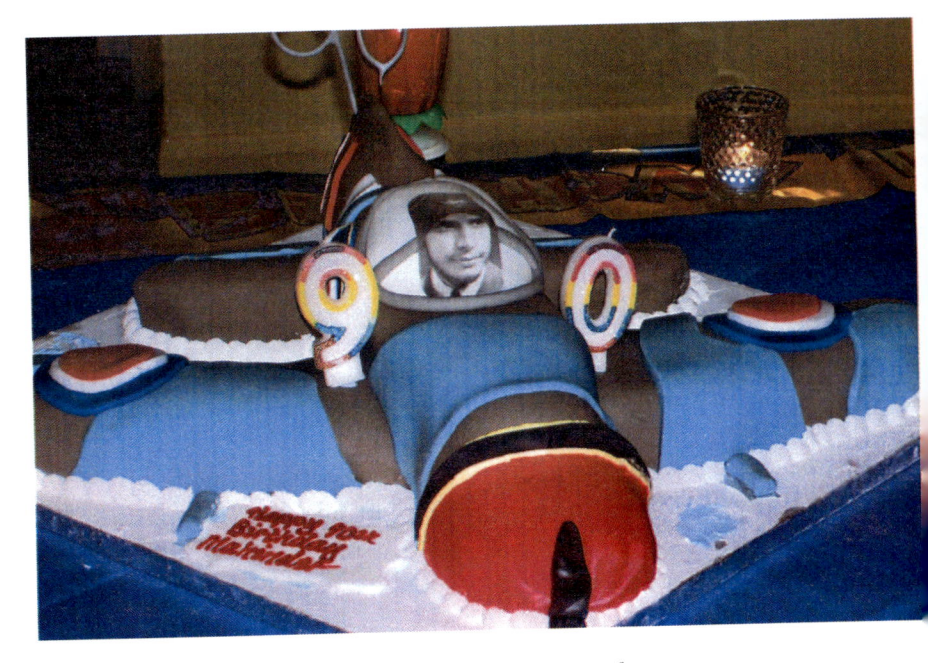

Pujji's ninetieth-birthday cake.

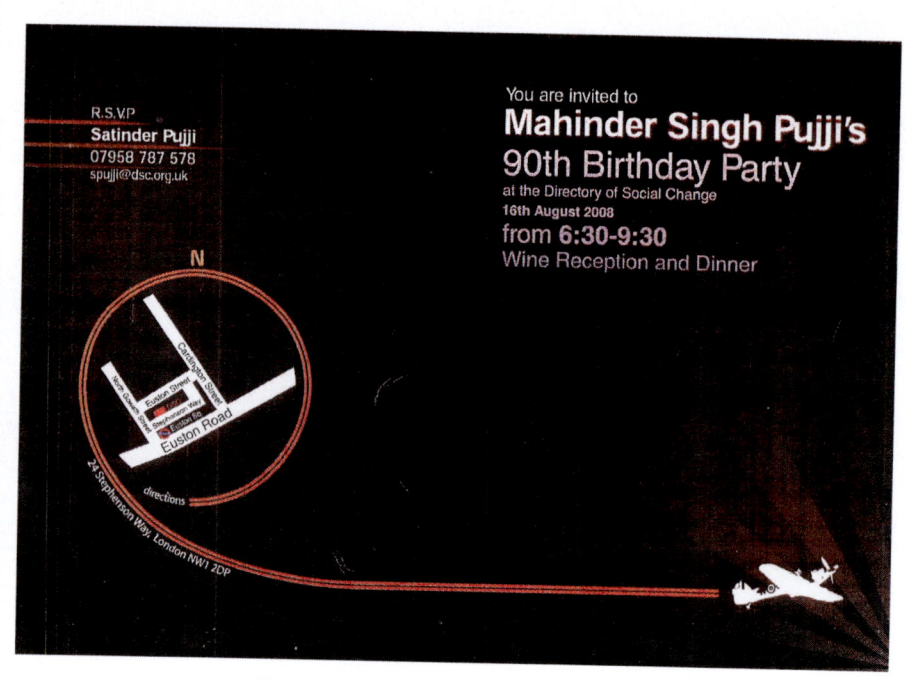

Pujji's ninetieth-birthday invitation.

Pujji is presented with an award by the police chief.

Pujji's ninetieth birthday party.

Pujji with his two grandchildren, Satish and Sharda, along with Raksha and Chani.

The Viscount Slim

House of Lords

Squadron Leader M S Pujji DFC, BA, LLB
14 Presentation House
The Grove
Gravesend
Kent DA12 1DX

3rd October 2008

Dear Mohinder,

I apologies for being out of touch for so long but I have been abroad and only returned the other day. I was so sad to miss your 90th birthday party and congratulate you on obtaining the great age you have and I wish you a very belated Happy Birthday. I read with interest your outstanding career and I love that photograph of you and Lady Mountbatten.

Just to remind you how highly my father thought of you and your Squadron and the particular operation you carried out I attach his own greeting card just so you realise that all Slims are happy to salute you.

You have done much for the Burma Star Association and I always feel especially good when you have stood beside me at important events. It demonstrates the great Indian Army and Air Force without whom the war in Burma would not have been won.

Keep going, I send you my warmest wishes and once more apologise for not being with you on that great day. Your photograph with Lady Mountbatten now sits on my desk and I speak with you every day.

Yours ever

John

Letter from Lord Slim.

Pujji is given a reception and helicopter flight by the police.

Pujji, his family and friends with the Mayor of Gravesend.

National

Heritage

RAF wartime exhibition celebrates the forgotten fewest of the Few

Air museum showcases black and Asian pilots who battled for Britain

Matthew Weaver

His daring exploits were typical of fighter pilots during the Battle of Britain: he shot down Messerschmits, was forced down twice and lost a lung flying at altitude. But how many other RAF squadron leaders used to keep a spare turban in their cockpits?

Mohinder Singh Pujji was one of 18 qualified Indian pilots to join the RAF in 1940. Now 90 he is the only one left to tell the tale and is still disgusted at the lack of recognition given to the role of black and Asian airmen and women during the war.

Pujji was treated as a hero in wartime Britain. He was ushered to the front of cinema queues and often treated to free meals in restaurants. But after the war films such as The Dam Busters presented a white-only view of the RAF – a fact that appalled him.

"The British people are foolish. They don't even know we Indians were there," he said.

In an attempt to put the record straight a new permanent exhibition was opened yesterday at RAF Cosford in Shropshire, called Diversity in the Royal Air Force. The launch comes in a week when Prince Harry's comments have reignited the debate about racism in the armed forces and the RAF is hoping that the exhibition will help to challenge negative perceptions by celebrating the racial diversity of its history.

It features men such as Indra Lal Roy, who fought in biplanes over first world war trenches or Princess Noor Inayat Khan, who served in the WAAF before being parachuted behind enemy lines to become the first woman wireless operator to infiltrate occupied France.

Stereotypes

The exhibition, in Cosford's fighting planes hangar, tells the story of the role of ethnic minorities in the RAF, using their own words and displays of their papers and medals.

It includes a personal combat report by Vincent Bunting, from Panama, after he shot down a Focke-Wulf. "I last saw the aircraft still spinning at 3,000 feet as it entered a cloud."

Al McLean, the museum's curator, said: "Too many of our visitors are white, over 50 and middle class. I want to appeal to more than just those people. This exhibition explains a side of our story that isn't recognised – that the RAF is not just a white public schoolboy occupation."

He added: "There is a comical stereotype of the RAF as full of tally-ho chaps. During the second world war there were lots of university students going into combat with 21 hours, but there were also lads from factories, and men from all over the Commonwealth who made up aircrews."

Pujji was the guest of honour at the launch of the exhibition, and tales of his wartime exploits stole the show.

"I loved flying and I wanted adventure," he said. "I didn't mind when I was shot at. It didn't frighten me at all."

He related that once his dashboard was shattered over France in a dogfight with a Messerschmitt by a bullet that had passed through four layers of his uniform. And in 1941 he was forced to land in the North African desert and was picked up by British troops. Awais Younis, 14, a pupil from Alexander High School in nearby Tipton, asked what plane Pujji had liked flying best.

Speaking within touching distance of the world's oldest Spitfire, he replied: "As a fighter pilot I liked Hurricanes best. Most people like Spitfires, but Hurricanes were easier to manoeuvre."

He later recounted how his turban had filled with blood when he was forced to land over France. After that he always carried a spare one. But he stopped wearing a turban in the 1960s. "Times changed," he said.

Pujji's son, Satinder, said his father's insistence on wearing a turban in combat had cost him a lung. It meant that he could not wear an oxygen mask and so one of his lungs was irreparably damaged at high altitude.

The exhibition acknowledges that many of the thousands of black and Asian members of the air force faced racial discrimination.

Asked if he had faced prejudice, Pujji said: "Only prejudice in my favour. In the restaurants people wouldn't charge me; in the picture houses they would let me go to the front of the queue." He added: "Everyone loved me and I fell in love with England. That was the mistake I made, I didn't realise it has changed now."

Recognition

Pujji retired to England after a career as a commercial pilot in India and now lives in Gravesend. The row about Prince Harry's comments he dismissed as "nonsense". "I've been called Paki hundreds of times, I didn't use to take offence. We used to call whites 'you lim'eys'. It's all nonsense."

What he is offended by is the way Indian airmen during the war have been forgotten. "Officially I don't receive any invitation to Remembrance Day services. They don't know I'm here."

But he is happy to be finally getting more recognition and to be back among the planes he fought in.

"Flying is my first love. It's always a pleasure to see the planes I was flying in."

Squadron leader Mohinder Singh Pujji, one of 18 qualified Indian pilots who joined the RAF in 1940, and the Hurricanes he flew (below)

Open skies Ethnic minorities in RAF

Indian nationals were commissioned into the Royal Flying Corps for the first time during WWI.

The "colour bar" or nationality disqualification was removed in the RAF in 1939; prior to this, signing up was limited to "British subjects of pure European descent".

An air ministry confidential order to commanding officers in June 1944 stated: "Any instance of discrimination on grounds of colour should be immediately and severely checked."

In 1999, Group Captain **André Dezonie** OBE became the first black officer ever to command an RAF base when he took control of RAF Wittering.

Currently 865 RAF personnel come from an ethnic minority background – 2.2% of the total, the MoD says.

Chief guest at the air museum at RAF Cosford.

world – a world he had helped to shape through his efforts in the war.

Pujji's had been a long and eventful career, and in 1970 he decided to retire, aged fifty-two. His professional involvement in aviation had come to an end, although he would still go gliding whenever he could. The government tried to tempt him again with a post as an aerodrome officer in Calcutta (or Kolkata, as it is now known), but he turned it down.

CHAPTER TEN

Heading for the West

It turned out to be the first of many retirements for Pujji. He liked to use the word, but a life of leisure rarely appealed to him for long. After all, there was always something that he had not yet tried. The era of his involvement in the aviation industry had finished as his legal career flourished.

He joined a law college, and, before long, he had qualified as a lawyer and started a practice in Bombay. His specialism was everything and anything. A year later he had enough money saved to send his twenty-year-old son, Satinder, to study in the US.

Considering he is one of the truly great aviators, Pujji gave his children a remarkably free rein to carve their own niches in life. There was no pressure to follow in their father's footsteps. In return, he received nothing but respect from his children.

"In India our children don't think what they're going to be," said Pujji. "When my son graduated he didn't have anything in mind. I asked him and he said, 'Dad, anything you want.'"

Satinder had caught the flying bug long before, most probably when his father took him up in a glider in New Delhi at the age of seven. He wanted to become a pilot, but he soon found out his eyesight was not good enough. "He wasn't despondent about it. He was like me: he was quite self-supporting," said Pujji, evidently proud of the qualities his son possesses.

However, Pujji was adamant his son should study in the US irrespective of the subject studied. So Satinder was sent to the

University of Nebraska to study engineering – a well-regarded profession in India. But the plan changed. Pujji soon received a letter from Satinder asking if he could do accountancy instead. It was the first step to a successful career in the profession, but he had to work for it. Pujji had not brought up his children to rely on him. Satinder studied hard and, when exams did not loom, he worked first in a petrol station and later in a Hilton hotel. He stayed abroad until 1977, when he came back with a wife – Manju – and a degree.

But two years into Satinder's studies, Pujji and Amrit wanted to visit him as part of a holiday. When they left for the trip, the thought that they would not return was inconceivable.

In a sense, Pujji was ready for the West. The Sikh tradition of never cutting your hair had already been broken after his crash-landing in Britain at the start of the war. Doctors had to shave off some of it to reach his head. "Once that is done, the faith is gone," said Pujji. In 1960, nearly twenty years later, he made the decision to stop wearing his turban – the headgear that had captured so many headlines in British newspapers and saved his life in combat.

A nervous Pujji called his father to break the news just before leaving for the gliding trip to Germany. Sohan Singh Pujji commanded enormous respect and was a noble man, strong in faith, bound with a sense of charity. Every morning, they used to visit the gurdwara and his father would help ferry other worshippers back home in his car afterwards. It was from him that Pujji inherited the principle of abstaining from drinking and smoking. Despite a lofty and demanding rank in the civil service, his father would make time every day to bring the family together, and he always ensured they had every convenience. Pujji was worried he would be upset at his decision to give up the turban.

"I told my father. He was horrified. He said, 'What are you on?' But then he said, 'You have lost faith so it doesn't really matter now.' He said, 'Do whatever you want to do.' I wasn't a practising Sikh, so it didn't mean anything," remembers Pujji. The telephone call had gone as well as it could have.

But Pujji still could not bear to tell his own wife of his decision yet. "When I packed my case for Germany my wife said, "You haven't packed your turbans." She packed a new one and, when she left, I took them out. I couldn't even tell her," said Pujji. Once he arrived in Germany, a like-minded Sikh – an Indian diplomat in Germany – helped him to cut his hair.

Another, far more personal, event had prepared him for his journey to the West: the death of his parents. His mother, Sant Kaur, had died in 1953, but very few people knew of it. As with the deaths of his colleagues in war, Pujji felt strongly about her passing but felt even more strongly that it was a private matter and that he must appear unfazed in public. He was notified of the terrible news by telegram while working in Dibrugarh. "My mother's death was very shocking. It was unexpected. But I didn't want others to know about it. I must be the only person in the world to be like that. It could be linked to all the death I saw in World War Two," said Pujji.

In 1971, his father, Sohan Singh, died. Pujji, who was working for Air India at the time, reacted in exactly the same way. He closed the door and grieved in private. Meanwhile, his public persona carried on, head held high. It was no reflection of a lack of emotional pain or love for those that had gone; it was more a reflection of his determination to keep going. Pujji noticed no small irony in the fact that he had spent the entire war preparing his parents for the event of his own death in action.

Despite these developments, Pujji and Amrit intended to go on a holiday and visit their son in Lincoln, Nebraska, stopping off in London on the way. But a meeting with old friends from the RAF Association, which Pujji wanted to join, dramatically changed their plans. Those at the association did more than let him join, they invited his family to come and live in England – a rare and exciting opportunity in those days.

"The whole idea of coming to Britain started there in 1974.

They said, 'You are already a DFC-decorated pilot; there will be no problem getting a visa.' So that's when I decided we could move from Bombay to London, as long as my wife agreed," remembers Pujji. It was as simple as that.

"Britain was always my favourite place because of the wonderful treatment I had during the war," he added. "I had very good memories of this country. We welcomed the idea of settling down here. It was the perfect opportunity, and we had to seize that opportunity."

While preparations were made, Pujji and his wife continued on to see Satinder in the US. They spent about a month there, excitedly debating all the possibilities that chance had thrown into their lap. They had, after all, left for a holiday, not to emigrate. They never used their return ticket to Bombay.

Pujji was entirely unprepared for setting up a new life in Britain. He didn't have a job or a house, he had very little English money and his idea of how British society worked was based on his wartime experiences more than thirty years earlier. It was just the kind of challenge a fifty-six-year-old Pujji cherished.

Pujji naturally gravitated towards where he felt most at home – the nearest airport. He stayed with relatives in Osterley, near Heathrow, West London. With his impressive credentials as an aerodrome officer in India counting for little in Britain, a management position was impossible. So Pujji applied to become an air traffic controller.

While he awaited the outcome of his application, he enjoyed a valuable opportunity to get back into the air, flying business executives around for a small outfit called Flight Aircraft Ltd. Things were beginning to look up.

The good news then came through that the job as an air traffic controller was his. The pay was pretty good, but he could still only rent a single room for himself and his wife in Hounslow. It was a far cry from the four-bedroomed bungalows the government gave him in India.

The change was difficult, but the hard-working Pujji valued his new start in life and appreciated what had been done for him. He supplemented his income by qualifying as a driving instructor and then passing his advanced driving test. His co-ordination and motor skills were as sharp as ever. Somehow, Pujji found teaching others to drive on the hectic streets of London quite relaxing. "This was a pleasure; there was no risk," he said with a smile.

Gliding was also never far from his mind and he soon made arrangements for a few unpowered pleasure trips above the green and pleasant land he had defended from the Germans more than three decades before. But the exhilaration of flying without an engine and being driven around in cars by complete novices was not enough, so at the age of sixty Pujji took up Hang-Gliding at weekends.

"I was in Dunstable in Bedfordshire and did a course in Hang-Gliding. It's much more dangerous than my previous pursuits – you jump from a hill," said Pujji. "It was just adventure that made me take it up. I went from flying to gliding to this. Flying was an adventure. In fact, all my life has been an adventure."

His extreme-sports career was cut short after just six months when his sports club got the jitters. "I had to give it up for one main reason," remembers Pujji. "When you land you have to bring your heavy equipment back. After one trip I found that a little hard to do. I was a manager at the time, and I got one of my employees to come with me and take my equipment. The club didn't like that and said I was too old. At that age you just can't carry all that stuff up a hill."

Nevertheless, Pujji continued to defy his age, achieving more during his pensioner years than many do in a lifetime. Following the expertise gained in India, he decided to take a British law course, and a year later he qualified as a solicitor. "It was just a case of learning English law," Pujji said simply. But rising to the top in legal circles took just too long for a man moving as fast as Pujji. "I was told I would earn £60 a week and would have to work under another barrister for two years," he said. This did not suit Pujji, so he only used his legal expertise to advise a West End hotel that he had come to manage.

Pujji's life is testament to the worth of a life spent impressing people and doing your best by them. A managerial job at the Hotel Strand Continental had come about through a chance meeting on a London street with a lady named Lachmi. Pujji had first met her when she was a fourteen-year-old after he first arrived in Britain during the Blitz.

He disliked British food so much at the time that his commanding officer had loaned him the use of his personal plane to fly to Bath, in Somerset, where Lachmi and her parents lived. "I used to go to their house to have Indian meals and go flying," said Pujji. His first trip there was cause for embarrassment rather than celebration, however. Pujji accidentally sparked fears he had crashed somewhere en route to their house: because he could not find the airport he had instead landed in an isolated field.

As the war years passed, the two friends stayed in touch by postcards and telegrams sent across the world. Sometimes Lachmi wrote about the most apparently mundane or everyday matters, but her words spoke to Pujji of real life, of normal life. One message from Lachmi to Pujji in the Western Desert in December 1941 informed him that his car had been sold for £45 and that his puppy was being sent to her in Bath.

But the friends lost contact after the war, until now. The chance meeting revealed that Lachmi had since married one of the directors of the Hotel in Strand. "She asked me, 'What about accommodation for your family?' She spoke to her husband and I was offered the job of general manager. The air traffic control had good pay, but there was no accommodation. This offer was something I couldn't refuse. I was earning about £200 a week with free board and lodging – a three-bedroom flat on the top floor – so it was a very wonderful deal. And I was the boss. It makes all the difference," said Pujji.

Amrit was soon given a job there, and it proved to be the move that set them up in Britain, the one that saw them truly settle here. In 1979 Pujji invited Amrit's brother, Kaka Ji, and his wife, Chani, to join him running the hotel. As Pujji added, "Coming to Britain was a big change, but I was very lucky. For twenty-two years I was number one in airports in India, and, after a brief spell in air traffic control, I became number one in hotels here."

It was during this period Pujji learned that his sister Raksha's husband had died leaving five young children needing support.

Nagina, the eldest daughter, joined a college and also took a part-time job. Raksha and infant son Shiv came to live with Pujji in London. The other daughters, Indu, Rajni and Meenakshi, were admitted to a public boarding school in Dehradun, India.

In December 1983, Nagina married Surinder. They now have three children, Anita, Ajay and Angela. Indu married Jaswinder. They have one daughter, Jessica. Rajni married Gurcharan. They have two sons, Gogna and Vicky. Meenakshi married Raju. They have a daughter, Muskan, and a son, Arwin. Shiv married Jyoti.

Soon his children followed his success, bringing further happiness for Pujji and Amrit. Satinder had successfully trained to become an accountant and had met an English girl named Manju. In 1977 Satinder and Manju returned to England and settled in Kensington, West London. They later had two children: a son, Satish, born in 1986, and a daughter, Sharda, born in 1993.

The good news continued in 1978 with the announcement of the marriage of Pujji's daughter, Rita, in Bombay to Mobez. Rita was working for Air India as a stewardess at the time.

Pujji's eldest daughter, Veena, had already married at the age of sixteen to businessman Prem Gupta (it had been a young marriage because Veena was being approached to become a film actress and the besotted Prem was worried she would be whisked away to seek fame and fortune).

The ceremony had taken place in Jaipur in 1962, and she and Prem were now settled in a hill station in India called Kulu. So now all the Pujji children were settled – something that brought him much joy.

In 1982, Pujji retired for a second time, aged sixty-four. He could finally relax and enjoy his growing family and the privileges that years of hard work had brought him. But his retirement was set against the background of a changing society in London. The Asian community had been growing for years in the capital, and there was a need for the authorities to communicate effectively with it and understand its main cultural tenets. By this time, Pujji already had some standing in the community, and he had got to know officers in the police force.

Before long, he gained a licence and was hired by the Metropolitan Police as an official interpreter, working wherever there was a need. "They would call me to different places, whether it was Southall or somewhere else," remembers Pujji. "I had to attend courts also to interpret: local courts all over London and the High Court. They paid me very well and I enjoyed the work."

Pujji became a close confidant for police officers keen to ensure harmony between different cultures. "I became very popular with the community and the police. The British wanted to build bridges with a growing Muslim community," Pujji said. He also became chairman of the Undivided Indian Ex-Services Association, based in Southall, West London.

Even in his later years, Pujji still felt a keen sense of duty when it came to remembering the Second World War. He felt Asian veterans were being left out of VJ-day celebrations, and he won greater recognition for their role. His views were reported by a number of newspapers.

And Pujji could still pull in the occasional VIP. In 1991, Diana Princess of Wales came to visit him in Southall. He was also a regular on the guest list whenever the royal family wished to mark a wartime anniversary.

In 2000, Pujji was given the freedom of the London Borough of Newham 'in recognition of the distinguished public services rendered by [him] as a former serving officer in the RAF' and to ex-servicemen from the Asian community. It was the first time such an award had been made by the authority in fifteen years.

When Pujji moved out of London to Gravesend, Kent, the honours still flowed. The county council there also honoured him in a special ceremony.

In 2002, Pujji took a break from receiving honours, opting to give them instead. Pujji received a letter saying that he had been selected on the personal recommendation of HRH Prince Philip to represent the veterans of the Commonwealth as he is the most decorated Indian officer to have flown in the RAF during the Second World War. He presented a vignette to HRH Prince Philip, Duke of Edinburgh, to highlight the plight of ex-servicemen across the world. It was one of many meetings he had with the royal family. Pujji had the honour of being invited to meet the royal family on more than one occasion. The first time was in 1940 at Windsor Castle. He then met them in India, where he was invited by the Maharaja of Jaipur to attend a dinner party to welcome the royal family. He was invited, along with his son Satinder and niece Nagina, to a commemorative lunch at Buckingham Palace in 2005 to mark the sixtieth anniversary of the end of the war. The prime minister, Tony Blair, also requested his presence at a similar event at Horse Guards Parade. He met Prince Philip again later that year at a ceremony to mark VJ-day.

The same year Pujji was invited to attend an opening ceremony at the Hendon War Museum as their guest of honour.

It was not just adoration from the public that Pujji received. For his eighty-fourth birthday, he was flown to see his family in California, where 100 relatives had gathered from at least eight countries for a ceremony reminiscent of British TV show *This Is Your Life*. He was then presented with a magnificent plaque, the wording of which appears at the beginning of this book. The event was organised by Pujji's nephew, Dr Anandjit Singh, and his wife Elsie.

Back home, Pujji's typical dedication also saw him volunteer to work for the Victim Support group – something he continued to do after his third retirement, this time as an interpreter, in 2006.

In 2007 he was recognised by Kent Police for his bravery and personal commitment to Britain throughout his life. They made particular note of his 'humility and open demeanour'. At the end of his acceptance speech he was given a standing ovation.

The same year he was fêted twice in one week in Gravesend. As part of Black History Month he was given special recognition by both the police and Kent County Council. Through the decades, few have been as brave and done as much to cement community relations as Pujji, said community leaders. A headline in the *Gravesend Messenger* after the event read, 'What He Has Done, Most People Only Dream Of'.

"I just wanted to help the community," said a ninety-one-year-old Pujji, his passion for fighting for others undimmed.

EPILOGUE

Pujji now shares his time between relatives in California, Gravesend and across India. Family and friends are important to Pujji, and he has asked that those family members and ex-colleagues not yet mentioned be referred to and honoured in this book.

He would first like to offer thanks to Graham Russell, Dr Anandjit Singh, Keith Wyncoll, Nagina and son Satinder Pujji for inspiring him to have this book written.

Urmil is also a member of Pujji's extended family and so is Mahinder Pal Singh Pujji. Urmil has two sons, Sunny and Sandy. Sunny is now married to Nancy. Mahinder Pal is now a captain with Indian Airlines. They have twins, who are now also qualified pilots.

From the first group of Indian pilots to come across to Britain, Pujji would like to mention Manmohan Singh, G. B. Singh, Metha and Tarlochan Singh, who were all killed in action.

Pujji would have probably faded away during the Blitz had it not been for the Indian food and friendship provided by Chaya and Maya Sen Gupta, and their sister, Lachmi, in Bath. Pujji would also like to mention Prabhjot Kaur, a President's Award-winning artist, for her help and kindness during the war.

When fighting in the deserts of the Middle East, Nazir Ullah was a staunch colleague.

While fighting in Afghanistan and Burma, Pujji was very close to those he commanded. In particular he would like to mention

Asghar, Rafiq Bokhari, Noel, H. Moolgavkar and Latif. In Burma, it would have been impossible to carry out many of his duties without pilots such as Air Chief Marshal (retired) Moolgavkar.

Pujji's life was as exciting and full of new friendships after his air-force career as during it. Very special friends in India include Surinder Gill and Raj Mitroo, the first two women he personally trained to become glider pilots.

PUJJI'S FAMILY

Wife: Amrit

Daughters: Veena and Rita

Son: Satinder

Seven grandchildren: Nomita, Sangeeta, Sabina, Sameer, Sahil, Satish and Sharda.

Four great grandchildren: Anahita, Akshay, Karan and Malvika.